*What to D*O *Before* *"I D*O*"*

the modern couple's guide to marriage, money and prenups

By Nihara Choudhri
Attorney at Law

SPHINX® PUBLISHING
AN IMPRINT OF SOURCEBOOKS, INC.®
NAPERVILLE, ILLINOIS
www.SphinxLegal.com

First Edition: 2004
Third Printing: May, 2005

Published by: **Sphinx® Publishing, An Imprint of Sourcebooks, Inc.®**

<u>Naperville Office</u>
P.O. Box 4410
Naperville, Illinois 60567-4410
630-961-3900
Fax: 630-961-2168
www.sourcebooks.com
www.SphinxLegal.com

This publication is designed to provide accurate and authoritative information in regard to the subject matter covered. It is sold with the understanding that the publisher is not engaged in rendering legal, accounting, or other professional service. If legal advice or other expert assistance is required, the services of a competent professional person should be sought.

From a Declaration of Principles Jointly Adopted by a Committee of the American Bar Association and a Committee of Publishers and Associations

This product is not a substitute for legal advice.

Disclaimer required by Texas statutes.

Library of Congress Cataloging-in-Publication Data

Choudhri, Nihara K.
  What to do before "I do" : the modern couple's guide to marriage, money, and prenups / Nihara K. Choudhri.-- 1st ed.
     p. cm.
  Includes index.
  ISBN 1-57248-451-9 (pbk. : alk. paper)
  1. Husband and wife--United States--Popular works. 2. Marital property--United States--Popular works. 3. Antenuptial agreements--United States--Popular works. I. Title.

KF524.Z9.C47 2004
346.7301'664--dc22
                                        2004020861

Printed and bound in the United States of America.

VP — 10 9 8 7 6 5 4 3

DEDICATION

To Trin, with love.

Contents

Rule #5: Take care of your prenuptial agreement well in advance of your wedding

Rule #6: Make sure that your prenuptial agreement is fair to your spouse-to-be

Rule #7: Update your prenuptial agreement regularly during your marriage

Divorce Provisions
Death Provisions
Money Management Provisions
Insurance Provisions
Lifestyle and Other Miscellaneous Provisions

An Introduction to Zack and Skye
Zack and Skye's Financial Disclosure
The Terms of Zack and Skye's Prenuptial Agreement
The Final Document: Zack and Skye's Prenuptial Agreement

When to Consider a Postnup

Introduction

When a date has been set and the invitations have been ordered, the last thing most couples have on their minds is the legal and financial side of marriage. Who will be responsible for the tax bill? What happens if one of you dies without a will? How will the house be divided in the event of a divorce? Almost no one—not even the most hard-nosed lawyer—enjoys thinking about debt, divorce, and death when wedding bells are chiming.

Like it or not, however, marriage is as much a legal and financial relationship as it is a romantic one. Once you walk down that aisle and exchange your vows, you and your soon-to-be spouse will have a whole new set of rights and responsibilities with respect to one another that you did not have before. Most people, however, do not learn about the legal and economic side-effects of marriage until the unexpected happens—when it is far too late to protect themselves or the people they love. Many people would have done things very differently had they known of the legal and financial consequences of marriage *before* tying the knot. Look at some of the following examples.

Adam, Evelyn, and the Perils of Married Filing Jointly

Evelyn and Adam filed their taxes jointly during their marriage. Thanks to the success of Evelyn's business, the couple enjoyed an extravagant lifestyle. Adam let Evelyn handle the family finances—including the tax returns—because Evelyn was much better at crunching the numbers. Several years into their marriage, the Internal Revenue Service audited the couple's tax returns and concluded that Evelyn had been dramatically underreporting her income. Adam was stunned to learn that he was equally on the hook for several hundred thousand dollars in tax liabilities and penalties, even though Evelyn was the one who had prepared their tax returns and underreported her business income. Had Adam known about the risks of filing his tax returns jointly with Evelyn, he would have made sure to file his tax returns separately throughout their marriage.

Jennifer, Paul, and the Murky Waters of Marital Property

Jennifer was frugal and hardworking, careful to save as much money as possible for a rainy day. Paul was a spendthrift with a slight tendency towards gambling. Because Jennifer was concerned about Paul's approach to money, she kept her earnings entirely separate, in a savings account in her name only. At the end of their nine-year marriage, Paul had saved only $5,000, while Jennifer had saved over $100,000 on nearly the same salary. When Paul filed for divorce, Jennifer was sure that she would be able to keep her savings free and clear. After all, she was the one who had saved and scrimped while Paul had spent. Jennifer was shocked to learn that her $100,000 was marital property, which she would have to share with Paul upon their divorce. Had Jennifer known this earlier, she would have been sure to ask Paul to sign a prenuptial agreement providing that their respective earnings would constitute separate property in the event of a divorce.

Collin, Sara, and the Unexpected Consequences of the Elective Share

Collin had three children from a previous marriage when he met Sara, an heiress to a huge ketchup fortune. Collin's will provided that all of his assets would go to his children when he died. Because Sara was independently wealthy, Collin saw no need to update his will after his marriage to Sara. Collin died of a heart attack just three weeks after their wedding. Collin's children rightfully expected that they would get all of their father's assets, as his will provided. The children were astonished to learn that Sara was entitled to one-third of their father's assets, even though his will made no provision for her. Had Collin known that Sara had an automatic right to a portion of his estate regardless of the terms of his will, he would have been certain to ask Sara to sign a written waiver of those rights, either before or soon after their marriage.

ॐ ॐ ॐ

As you can see, saying *I do* without first learning how marriage affects your legal and economic rights is risky business. Marriage is a binding legal contract, one with *plenty* of hidden fine print. You owe it to yourself and those you love to take the time to understand the terms.

This book will provide you with an easy-to-follow explanation of the legal and financial consequences of marriage. You will learn how marriage affects your rights regarding debt, divorce, and death. You will also get lots of valuable tips on how to avoid common pitfalls and protect yourself. (For example, you will learn how to keep your assets safe from your spouse's creditors.)

This book will then introduce you to a powerful alternative to the default marriage rules—the prenuptial agreement. Prenuptial agreements allow couples to write their own vows, so to speak. This book will help you understand why you might want to consider a prenuptial agreement; what you can and cannot cover in your prenuptial agreement; and, how to ensure that your prenuptial agreement is as rock-solid as possible.

If you are uncomfortable with the idea of a prenuptial agreement, rest assured that this book is not an advocacy piece for them. The goal of this book is simply to ensure that you embark on your marriage with your eyes open to the legal and financial ramifications of your decision. Reading this book will hopefully spare you from some unpleasant surprises down the road, and help you and your soon-to-be spouse make well-informed financial decisions at every step of your journey ahead. Plan for every possibility, but hope for the very best—and may the joys of your married life far exceed even your wildest expectations.

A Quick Note to Readers

To help you understand the many different concepts covered in this book, examples are provided wherever possible. You will notice that a number of the characters in the examples are fabulously wealthy: some are baronesses, others are heirs to major fortunes, and one or two are tremendously successful real estate mavens. Using wealthy characters makes it easier to illustrate some of the issues addressed in this book. It packs more of a punch to say that someone would lose $200,000—rather than just $2,000—by choosing one course of action over another. This is not to imply that only the very rich need to think about the financial and legal consequences of tying the knot. Usually, the very wealthy have enough lawyers and financial advisors on their staffs to do all the planning for them. It is the *regular Joes*—people like you and me—who need to be reminded to focus on the decidedly unromantic, practical side of marriage.

You will also notice that every example in the book involves a heterosexual couple. This is not in any way intended to reflect the author's view as to whether or not same-sex couples should be entitled to the privileges (and disadvantages!) of the institution of marriage. Rather, the examples are limited to heterosexual couples because as of the time of the writing of this book, same-sex couples could not marry under the laws of most states.

I

For Richer, For Poorer: Debt and the Married Couple

While marrying for money has long since fallen out of style, there is no denying that money still has a lot to do with marriage. The fact is, who you marry has a tremendous impact on your present and future financial circumstances. If you marry someone with good money management skills and a sound approach to saving and investing, your chances for having a balanced budget and building a healthy *nest egg* during the course of your marriage are very good. If, on the other hand, you marry someone with far more liabilities than assets, you could end up losing your shirt to your spouse's creditors unless you are careful.

This chapter helps you understand why you should concern yourself with debts and liabilities when going into a marriage. This chapter also explains what you need to know about your soon-to-be spouse's debts and liabilities before tying the knot. It gives you helpful tips on what you should think about before taking out joint debts—such as a mortgage loan—with your spouse. Although there is no way to plan perfectly for the road ahead, following the advice in this chapter can help ensure that you and your spouse steer clear of some surprisingly common financial pitfalls.

The Deal with Debt

You might think that debt is really no big deal. After all, when people are just starting out in life, it is natural that their liabilities outweigh their assets for a few years until their salaries catch up with their lifestyle. There is certainly some truth to this notion. It is certainly true that properly managed debt, used for fruitful purposes (like a college education), is an incredibly useful financial tool. When people take on more debt than they can handle, however, very bad things can happen. Even if you have been a model of fiscal discipline, your excellent track record could get bungled if you marry someone who has taken on too much debt too quickly, without a good debt management plan.

This may all make sense to you in theory, but as a practical matter, why should you *really* concern yourself with debt when you are about to take the plunge into matrimony? First, debt can get in the way of your personal and financial dreams. Being saddled with too much debt can chain you to a job you hate or put a wrench in your plans to buy a new home or travel the world. Second, mismanaged or delinquent debt can sap much of the joy out of your married life.

Creditors have a *tremendous* amount of power to make your life miserable if you fail to meet your repayment obligations. This power extends beyond just overloading your answering machine and mailbox with nasty messages from collection agencies. Creditors can, for example:

- freeze your bank accounts, leaving you (and your hard-earned money) out in the cold;
- repossess your house or your car, sending you back to the student life of renting and taking public transportation; and,
- garnish your wages, taking up to a whopping twenty-five percent of your take-home pay.

The point of all this is not to scare you, but to impress upon you the importance of taking debts and liabilities *very* seriously. You should be extremely candid about your debts and liabilities with your soon-to-be spouse, and you should make sure your beloved is just as frank with you. Ideally, the two of you should sit down and come up with a realistic debt management plan, both for paying off current debt and for taking on future debt. This does not necessarily mean that you need to pool your finances and share responsibility for one another's debts. Depending on your particular circumstances and preferences, you and your soon-to-be spouse might decide that you are each solely liable for your own debts and liabilities and that you will never take on joint debts during your marriage. The exact plan that you decide on is not all that important. What *is* important is that you and your beloved actually have a plan when it comes to debts and liabilities.

Know What You are Getting Into

Few things in life are as unromantic as sitting down with your soon-to-be spouse and talking turkey about finances. Even for the most open of couples, sharing the dirty details of one another's checkbooks and credit card accounts can lead to an awkward conversation.

However, unless you are willing to risk some pretty unpleasant (not to mention costly) surprises down the line, you and your soon-to-be spouse should find the time to sit down and share the deepest secrets of your financial lives. So get yourselves a nice bottle of wine, sit in front of a roaring fire, and get down to the nitty-gritty of one another's debts and liabilities.

Be sure that you ask your beloved about each and every possible debt and liability, including:

- ◆ student loans;
- ◆ credit card debt;
- ◆ mortgage and home equity loans;
- ◆ car loans;
- ◆ margin loans from brokerage accounts;
- ◆ pension and 401(k) loans;

- outstanding tax liabilities;
- personal loans from friends and family members;
- small business loans for which he or she is personally liable;
- pending lawsuits; and,
- outstanding money judgments.

Familiarize yourselves with one another's credit and bill payment history. For example, has your spouse-to-be ever filed for bankruptcy or fallen more than several months behind on his or her student loan payments? You should also talk about expected future liabilities. For example, if your beloved is in a high-liability profession, such as surgery or obstetrics, or is your beloved is a small business owner who may personally guarantee business loans?

If it turns out that your future spouse has large amounts of personal debt, or is in a high-liability profession, you should seriously consider keeping your assets entirely separate from his or her assets. (For example, by putting only your name on the title of your new vacation home on the beach.) This way, your spouse's creditors can only reach his or her assets in the event of a default or a large judgment for money damages. Your assets will remain safe and untouchable. The same holds true in reverse. If you are the one with the high debt burden or liability exposure, then you will be financially better off as a couple if your spouse keeps his or her assets separate from yours.

Joint Debt

Chances are high that you and your soon-to-be spouse, like most couples, will end up incurring joint debt in some form or another at some point during your marriage. For example, you might take out a mortgage in both names to purchase your very first home. Or you might open up a joint credit card account so that you can have the convenience of one monthly bill reflecting all of your living expenses.

If you decide to undertake any type of joint liability with your spouse, you should bear in mind that you will be personally responsible for the *full amount* of any debt that is taken out in both of your names until the debt is repaid in full, regardless of whether your spouse earns more money than you do or was primarily responsible for incurring the debt. You will continue to be fully responsible for your joint debts, even if you and your spouse divorce and a judge assigns all of your debts to your spouse. This is because even a divorce court does not have the authority to alter the terms of a preexisting contract between you and a lender.

EXAMPLE

Seth and Molly bought a rambling Victorian home in Cape May two years after they were married. Seth could not have been happier in the house. He delighted in spending his weekends refinishing the original hardwood floors and repairing the rusty plumbing. Molly, on the other hand, hated the creaky stairs and the drafty windows. Over time, she also grew to hate spending time with Seth, and the two filed for divorce just before their fifth anniversary.

Molly's lawyer recommended that she and Seth immediately sell the house and share the proceeds. Because Molly knew that the house was dear to Seth, she could not bear the thought of forcing him to sell it. Unfortunately for Molly, Seth could only keep the house if Molly's name remained on the mortgage and the deed. (Seth's income was too low to enable him to refinance the mortgage in his name only.) This meant that she continued to be liable to the bank for the monthly mortgage payments and was fully responsible if Seth defaulted on the loan.

Everything went smoothly at first. Seth made the mortgage payments on time and in full, and Molly moved on with her life. A few years later, however, Molly received a notice in the mail informing her that Seth had fallen behind on his mortgage payments and the bank was now foreclosing on the home. Even though it was Seth who had failed to make the mortgage payments, Molly's perfect credit rating was destroyed. Because her name had remained on the mortgage, she remained liable for the full amount of the mortgage. After the foreclosure, Molly could no longer even qualify for a credit card, much less a mortgage on a new home.

Because of the risks associated with incurring liabilities jointly with your spouse, you should be extremely careful before leaping headfirst into debt with your beloved. The following are a few things to consider before undertaking certain types of joint liabilities with your spouse.

JOINT CREDIT CARD ACCOUNTS

You should not open a joint credit card account with your spouse unless you are completely confident that your spouse will use the credit card sensibly and will not ring up unnecessary credit card debt. If you like the convenience of having a joint credit card account, but are nervous about one day being hit with a monster-sized credit card bill, then talk to your credit card provider about placing a manageable limit on your line of credit. That way, you will know in advance what your maximum liability could be if it turns out that your spouse relies on plastic a bit more than you would like. If you decide to go forward with a joint credit card account, monitor the account closely (even if your spouse is the one who manages the household finances), to ensure that you are not racking up too much in credit card debt and you are paying your monthly bills on time.

JOINT MORTGAGE LIABILITY

Almost every couple dreams of owning a home together. Whether you and your beloved envision a beachside bungalow in Florida or a condo in

Manhattan, you are probably going to end up taking out a mortgage loan to make your home ownership dreams a reality. Because few commitments in life are as binding and as serious as taking out a mortgage, you should make sure you fully understand what you are getting into before signing on the dotted line for a joint mortgage loan with your spouse.

First, you must always bear in mind that your mortgage payment history is going to make or break your credit report. Making your monthly mortgage payments on time and in full is going to be a very good sign to future lenders that you and your spouse honor your commitments to repay debt. If, on the other hand, you take out more mortgage debt than you can handle and have difficulty keeping up to date with your mortgage payments, then both of your credit histories will be destroyed.

There are two steps you should take to ensure that your mortgage loan is always in good standing. The first is to be careful that you do not take on a greater mortgage burden than you can reasonably afford. While there is something to be said for stretching yourselves to buy a comfortable first home, make sure that you do not *overextend* yourselves just for an extra bedroom or a slightly better view. The second is to take advantage of the *direct debit option* offered by your mortgage lender. This option allows your mortgage payment to be automatically debited from your account each month, so there will never be any question as to whether you paid your bill in full or on time.

Second, you should think about what would happen to your home if you or your spouse died prematurely. If either of you would be unable to afford the monthly mortgage payment on your own, you should give some serious thought to purchasing *mortgage-canceling life insurance* (which is just life insurance in the amount necessary to pay down the full outstanding balance of your mortgage). In the event that one spouse dies, the insurance proceeds could be used to pay down the mortgage and enable the surviving spouse to remain in the home and hold on to all the memories it contains.

Finally, you should know that if you and your spouse divorce after you have had children together, there is a reasonable possibility that a court would allow the spouse with custody to remain in the home until the children reach 18. Unless the spouse with custody has a high enough income to qualify for the mortgage alone or can otherwise refinance the loan, the noncustodial spouse's name will remain on the mortgage until the house is ultimately sold. This means that the noncustodial spouse will continue to be liable for the full amount of the mortgage, and be personally responsible for any late payments or defaults on the mortgage loan, until the house is ultimately sold. The noncustodial spouse may also be unable to purchase another home during this time, because he or she may have already maxed out his or her credit capacity through the first mortgage. To avoid this type of situation, it would be best if you and your soon-to-be spouse could come to some agreement in advance as to what will happen to your home in the event of a divorce.

CONSOLIDATING STUDENT LOANS

If you and your spouse are students or recent graduates, you may find yourselves swimming in student loan debt. To lower your monthly payments and streamline your debts, the two of you might decide to consolidate your student loans. You should be aware that doing so will likely render you personally liable for your spouse's student loan debts (check the agreement with your loan company for exact details on this). This means that even if your marriage goes south or your spouse passes away, you will continue to be responsible for the full amount of your spouse's student loan debt in addition to your own.

You should also know that student loan debt—unlike most other forms of personal debt—is very difficult to discharge in bankruptcy. So think long and hard before you take on major additional liabilities for the sake of administrative convenience or a small interest rate discount.

Marital Debt

Unless you and your spouse-to-be sign a prenuptial agreement specifying otherwise, almost all of the debt that you and your spouse incur during your marriage—whether in joint names or in separate names—will likely be considered *marital debt* in the event of a divorce. This means that a court will divide that debt between the two of you at the end of a marriage, much in the same way it divides your marital assets. Different courts have different ways of apportioning marital debt. Some courts will divide debts and liabilities equally between the spouses. Other courts will assign debts and liabilities based on who incurred them and the circumstances of the case. Regardless of how a court in your state would handle marital debts and liabilities, keep the concept of marital debt in mind, because it could have the effect of reducing your share of marital assets in the event of a divorce.

EXAMPLE

Anthony and Caroline argued almost endlessly about money throughout their four-year marriage. While Caroline saved as much as possible in hopes of one day having enough for a down payment on a house, Anthony spent his paychecks faster than he could earn them.

A particularly sore spot in their relationship was Anthony's Ford Mustang, which Caroline viewed as nothing more than a cash pit. Every few weeks, Anthony purchased some new accessory or financed some new repair job for the Mustang. When Anthony splurged on a new paint job for the Mustang for the third time in four years, Caroline decided she had enough and filed for divorce.

The judge awarded Caroline 70% of the net marital estate (meaning the marital assets less the marital debt). Caroline was pleased with the outcome until she realized that Anthony had rung up nearly ten thousand dollars in Mustang-related debt during their marriage, while their total savings during their marriage amounted to only twenty thousand dollars. Because of the debt that Anthony had rung up during their marriage, Caroline walked away from their marriage with only seven thousand dollars.

Tax Liability

The tax laws are somewhat unfriendly towards married couples. First, there is the much-detested *marriage penalty*, whereby married couples filing jointly end up paying slightly higher taxes than similarly-situated unmarried couples. As if that were not enough, the tax laws also hold spouses filing jointly *completely* responsible for one another's tax understatements. In other words, if your spouse fails to accurately report his or her income on your joint tax return, then you are just as responsible as your spouse for any resulting tax liability, as well as any interest or penalties assessed by the Internal Revenue Service (IRS).

EXAMPLE

Michelle, a freelance writer, had always filed her tax returns jointly with her husband, Alex. Alex ran a very successful landscaping business and was responsible for caring for the shrubs and hedges of some of the town's most famous residents. While Michelle knew that Alex's business was quite lucrative and facilitated their luxurious lifestyle, she had never really concerned herself with the actual profit and loss figures. (Math had never been Michelle's forte.) Michelle just assumed that Alex was reporting his income accurately on their joint tax returns and signed their joint tax returns each year without much thought.

When the couple was audited several years into their marriage, the IRS discovered that Alex had been dramatically underreporting the business's income and assessed the couple with nearly three hundred thousand dollars in unpaid tax liabilities. Michelle was shocked when she heard the news of the IRS's assessment of back taxes. She was even more stunned to learn that she was just as responsible as Alex for the thousands of dollars in tax liability.

There is no statute of limitations on *tax fraud*. This means that the IRS can come after you and your spouse even five or ten years after you file your tax returns for underreporting your income.

The IRS recognizes that it is not always fair to hold both spouses equally liable for one spouse's misstatement of income. Accordingly, the IRS will relieve one spouse from responsibility for the other spouse's tax underreporting in very limited circumstances. Pursuant to what is known as *Innocent Spouse Relief*, one of the main avenues for relief for blameless spouses, the IRS can let the innocent spouse off the hook if that spouse can demonstrate that:

◆ he or she did not know, and *had no reason to know*, that there was a tax understatement on the joint tax return and

◆ it would be unfair to hold him or her liable for the tax deficiency, given all of the facts and circumstances of the case.

If there was reason for the supposedly blameless spouse to suspect that tax underreporting was taking place—for example, if a couple lived like millionaires but only listed a few hundred thousand dollars of income on their joint tax returns—then the IRS will likely deny *Innocent Spouse Relief*.

Because tax liability is no joking matter, you should not file your tax returns jointly with your spouse unless you are confident that your spouse is reporting his or her income accurately. You should be especially vigilant if your spouse is self-employed or takes much of his or her income *off the books*. If you have any reservations at all about your spouse's honesty with respect to the IRS, the safest course of action is to file your tax returns separately.

Filing your tax returns separately may not be a complete solution to the problem if you happen to live in a community property state. Depending on the rules in your state, you may be required to report half of all income earned by both you and your spouse on your separate tax return, because this income is considered to have been earned by the *community*. Check with your accountant or tax lawyer about the best route to take if your state follows community property laws and you are concerned about filing jointly with your spouse.

2

For Better, For Worse: Till Divorce Do Us Part

The sad reality is that divorce is a significant possibility for even the most devoted of couples. Current statistics indicate that half of all first marriages end in divorce, with 60% of second marriages suffering the same fate. With such staggering divorce rates, it dangerously naïve to embark on a marriage without contemplating what will happen in the event your marriage fails.

This very hefty chapter will explain the rules governing divorce, covering everything from the grounds for divorce to the division of marital property to spousal support. Hopefully, your marriage will stand the test of time and these rules will never apply to you. If the unthinkable does happen, however, you will be in a much better position to protect your rights if you take a little time *before* getting married to familiarize yourself with the divorce laws.

The State of Divorce

These days, most couples end up moving to a different state at some point during their marriages. A couple might get married in one state, live for several years in another state, and finally settle down in a third state. Which state's divorce laws would apply if that couple were to get divorced? This is a fairly important question because the divorce laws vary considerably from state to state.

People are often surprised to learn that the laws of the state in which they live at the end of their marriage will apply if they divorce, not the laws of the state in which they were married.

EXAMPLE

David and Suzanne were married in New York and lived there for ten years. When David landed a job with a powerful Silicon Valley company, the couple moved to a sun-filled condominium in Cupertino, California. David worked very long hours and Suzanne felt increasingly isolated, miles away from her friends and family. Their marriage unraveled under the pressure. Suzanne eventually filed for divorce. David was rather unhappy to learn that California's divorce laws applied, rather than New York's divorce laws. What difference did it make? Under California law, Suzanne was automatically entitled to one-half of everything David earned during their marriage. New York law only guaranteed Suzanne an equitable share of David's marital earnings—which could mean less than half, if a court decided that was fair.

As a practical matter, it is not enough to understand the divorce laws of the state in which you and your spouse marry. You should also learn the divorce laws of any state you and your spouse move to during your marriage. But even this may not be enough, since the divorce laws change from time to time. If you would rather know in advance what will happen in the event that you and your spouse divorce—instead of letting your fate be decided by whatever laws are in effect in the state in which you happen to live at the time—then you might want to consider a prenuptial agreement.

The Grounds for Divorce

While unmarried people may leave their lovers—for any reason or no reason at all—whenever they please, married folks can only exit their marriages if they have *grounds* (a legal reason) to obtain a divorce. For better or for worse, marriage creates a legal bond between you and your significant other.

Once upon a time, you could only divorce your spouse if he or she had done something wrong—like cheating on you or abandoning you. Those days are long gone. Now, every state offers some type of *no-fault grounds* for divorce. In most states, you can obtain a divorce from your spouse simply on the grounds that the two of you have *irreconcilable differences*. A small number of states still require that you and your spouse be formally separated for a certain period of time (usually one year) before it will grant you a no-fault divorce.

The no-fault grounds for divorce have made it much easier to obtain a divorce than it used to be. To obtain a divorce on grounds of *irreconcilable differences*, for example, all a judge will usually require is a sworn statement from the person who wants the divorce that the marriage has broken down and there is no reasonable possibility of reconciliation. A divorce will then be granted, even if the other spouse opposes the divorce and has never been abusive or unfaithful.

Why does it sound so easy to obtain a no-fault divorce in most states these days? The reason is that almost all divorce judges recognize that there is no real point in forcing spouses to remain married when one spouse wants out.

In addition to the no-fault grounds for divorce, nearly all states also offer *fault grounds*. The most common fault grounds for divorce are adultery, abandonment, and cruel and inhuman treatment. Filing for divorce on fault grounds packs far less of a punch than it once did. In the days of fault-based divorces, courts would punish the guilty spouse by giving him or her a smaller share of marital property or a larger alimony bill. Things have changed a great deal since then. In most states, fault plays no role whatsoever in marital property division or alimony decisions. As a practical matter, this can mean that a philandering or physically abusive spouse walks away from a marriage with the same amount of marital property as a devoted and doting spouse.

EXAMPLE

> Sandra married Rob, her high school sweetheart, at the age of 23. She planned her entire life around Rob, moving coasts to accommodate his career and giving up her pursuit of an advanced degree in order to stay home with their three children. Fifteen years into their marriage, Rob stunned Sandra by asking for a divorce. Rob explained that he had fallen in love with someone else and no longer wished to be with Sandra. Shattered, Sandra spent months in denial before finally going to see a lawyer. Sandra was sure that since Rob had cheated on her, she would be entitled to a very large share of the property they had accumulated together, plus a sizeable amount in alimony. Sandra could not believe her ears when her lawyer told her that Rob's adultery was entirely irrelevant for the purposes of marital property division and alimony under the laws of her state.

The Basics of Marital Property Division

Before a couple marries, the question of who owns what is relatively straightforward. Everything in your name is yours; everything in your significant other's name is his or hers; and everything in both names is yours to share. If you and your onetime-beloved decide to go your separate ways, you each keep the money you have saved up in your own separate accounts and you each walk away with sole and complete responsibility for your own debts (assuming you have not entered into some other binding agreement, such as a joint credit card or a car loan). After a couple marries, each person's property rights change dramatically.

When a couple divorces, each spouse is entitled to a share of all *marital property* (called *community property* in some states). Different states have different rules regarding what counts as marital property and what counts as separate property. The general rule in all states, however, is that *everything you and your spouse earn during your marriage counts as marital property.* This is true even if you and your spouse each maintain separate bank accounts and keep all of your property in your name only.

EXAMPLE

Dennis and Annette were married for ten years. Dennis loved Annette dearly, but he was concerned about the possibility of losing his shirt in a divorce. To protect himself (or so he thought), Dennis deposited half of each of his paychecks into a joint account with Annette and the other half into a savings account in his name only. Dennis thought that his savings account would be his to keep, free and clear, in the event that Annette walked out on him.

As it turned out, Annette left Dennis for an aspiring actor she met over martinis at the tennis club. Annette's divorce lawyer demanded that Dennis give Annette a share of the money in his savings account, claiming that the savings account constituted marital property. Dennis was floored when his own lawyer informed him that Annette's lawyer was right—the savings account was in fact marital property. Why? Because *all* of the money Dennis earned during their marriage constituted marital property, regardless of the fact that some of the money was kept in Dennis's name only.

Determining what counts as marital property is only the first step in marital property division. The second step is actually dividing the marital property between husband and wife. In some states, such as California, each spouse automatically gets half of all marital property at the end of a marriage. Most states, however, divide marital property *equitably*—or according to what is fair under the circumstances. This can mean that one spouse walks away with 75% of all marital property, for example, while the other spouse receives only 25% of the available marital property. Some states split the difference between the two systems, dividing marital property equally unless it would be inequitable—or unfair—to do so under the particular circumstances of the case.

This section will first explain what counts as marital property, and will then turn to the sometimes tricky question of what counts as separate property. Once you have learned the differences between marital property and separate property, this section will then help you understand how marital property is divided in a divorce. You will soon see that marital property division is a complicated subject. Still, it is definitely worth taking the time to understand the rules since marriage has such a significant impact on your property rights.

Understanding Marital Property

Only marital property is generally divided between a husband and wife at the end of a marriage. All other property—known as *separate property*—generally belongs to each spouse, free and clear of any claim by the other spouse, at the end of a marriage. The question of what counts as marital property and what counts as separate property is, therefore, extremely important.

In most states, marital property consists of all property that either spouse earns or acquires during the marriage. Marital property generally does *not* include:

♦ property earned or acquired by either spouse prior to the marriage;

♦ property either spouse received as a gift;

♦ property inherited by either spouse; and,

♦ property received by either spouse as compensation for a personal injury.

The concept of marital property is generally defined very broadly to include anything of value that either spouse earns or acquires during the marriage. For example, pensions, stock options, retirement benefits, businesses, professional goodwill, intellectual property, and even frequent flier miles can all count as marital property in the event of a divorce.

To help you understand what counts as marital property in most states, consider the following situation.

EXAMPLE

Trevor and Amanda were married for twenty-three years. Trevor had gone into the dry cleaning business a few years after he married Amanda and he owned three dry cleaning stores when Amanda filed for divorce. Trevor also had a sizeable retirement portfolio, which he had built up during his marriage. Amanda had inherited $200,000 from her godfather, which she kept in a separate account in her name only. Amanda and Trevor also owned a home and two cars together.

In this case, the marital property would consist of Trevor's three dry cleaning stores, Trevor's retirement portfolio, the home that Amanda and Trevor owned together, and their two cars. Amanda's inheritance would count as her separate property and would not be divided with Trevor as part of their divorce.

Sometimes, dividing only marital property and leaving separate property untouched can mean that one spouse walks away from a marriage with almost nothing. In recognition of this fact, courts in a few states will divide separate property in addition to marital property where it would be unfair to do otherwise.

Francesca and Roberto were married for fifteen years. Roberto did not work at all during the marriage because he was the recipient of a generous trust fund from his grandmother. Roberto earned enough income from the trust fund to cover the family's expenses and support his own luxurious tastes. Francesca worked as a part-time journalist during the marriage and managed to save nearly $75,000, despite her meager salary. Under the usual marital property/separate property rules, Roberto's trust fund would be entirely off-limits in a divorce because it was a gift from Roberto's grandmother, while Francesca's $75,000 in savings would be up for grabs because she earned that money during the marriage. A court in a state following the hybrid system of property division would be able to avoid such an unfair result by treating Roberto's trust fund as marital property. This would allow Francesca to keep her small savings and perhaps even obtain a small share of Roberto's trust fund assets.

Trying to keep track of what counts as marital property and what counts as separate property can get very confusing. Some states—such as Connecticut—avoid the whole problem by counting *all* property owned by both spouses at the end of a marriage as marital property. These states are sometimes referred to in divorce lingo as *kitchen sink states*, meaning that everything including the kitchen sink is up for grabs when a couple divorces. People living in *kitchen sink states* have reason to be extra cautious when tying the knot, particularly if they have substantial premarital assets or expect a sizeable inheritance.

Understanding Separate Property

In states that distinguish between marital property and separate property, the most common categories of separate property are:

- property acquired prior to marriage;
- gifts and inheritances; and,
- property received by either spouse as compensation for a personal injury.

Property that falls into any of these categories is usually off-limits in the event of a divorce provided that the property is kept in one spouse's name only and is not *commingled* with marital property during the marriage. (See the section entitled "The Importance of Keeping Separate Property Separate," page 27.) Each of the foregoing categories of property is discussed in more detail in this section. The question of how separate property appreciation and the income from separate property are handled in the event of a divorce is also addressed.

PROPERTY ACQUIRED PRIOR TO MARRIAGE
People are often surprised to learn that any property either spouse earned or otherwise acquired *before* the marriage counts as his or her separate property and is usually not divided in the event of a divorce.

EXAMPLE
Gina met Adrian, a retired real estate maven, while sailing in the Caribbean. Gina was enchanted by Adrian's deep blue eyes and his fabulous wealth. He owned a number of exclusive hotels in California and had homes all over the world. Gina said *yes* before Adrian even finished proposing. Their whirlwind romance lasted eight years, until Adrian announced that he was leaving Gina for his personal trainer. While Gina was quite upset about the personal trainer situation, she was glad that at least she had the good sense to marry a wealthy man. She assumed that she would be entitled to her share of Adrian's real estate portfolio, a tidy chunk of change that would enable her to

live comfortably for the rest of her life. Gina was utterly flabbergasted when her lawyer told her that Adrian's *entire* real estate
portfolio constituted his separate property because it was
acquired before his marriage to her. This meant that Gina was
not entitled to any part of Adrian's real estate portfolio upon
their divorce.

In the real world, the question of whether property was acquired
before or after the marriage is not always so black and white, since
property is sometimes paid for in part before the marriage and in part
during the marriage.

EXAMPLE

Harry and Christina lived together for five years before Harry
proposed. While they were engaged, Harry bought the house of
Christina's dreams, one complete with the ocean views and sun
deck that Christina had always envisioned. Both the house and
the mortgage were in Harry's name only. Harry and Christina
lived in the house together for the ten years they were married.
When Christina filed for divorce, she assumed that the house
constituted marital property, since they had lived in it together
for so long and Harry had made sizeable mortgage payments during their marriage. Harry assumed that the house constituted his
separate property, since he bought the house before his marriage
to Christina. Harry and Christina spent thousands of dollars in
legal fees and months in court litigating the issue of whether the
house constituted marital property. They finally settled out of
court, with each getting much less than he or she wanted.
Christina would have been far better off had she asked Harry to
sign a prenuptial agreement, providing that she would be entitled
to one half of the house's net value in the event of a divorce.

GIFTS AND INHERITANCES

Those who are fortunate enough to have wealthy and generous bene-
factors are often quite relieved to learn that most states count inheritances and gifts as separate property, as long as the inheritance or gift
was made to one spouse only. When gifts or bequests are made to both
spouses together, however, the gifts constitute marital property.

EXAMPLE

Dixon and Katie inherited a small chateau in the south of France
from Dixon's eccentric but endearing Aunt Madeleine. Aunt
Madeleine's last will and testament provided that the house
should go to *my nephew, Dixon, despite his pessimistic approach to life, and his
delightful wife, Katie, who has always been like a daughter to me.* The chateau
was a dream come true for Katie and Dixon. They vacationed
there each summer and rented the chateau out during the rest of
the year for a healthy sum.

Dixon and Katie's life remained as dreamy as the chateau itself
until Dixon decided that Katie's optimistic spirit was grating on
his nerves. Dixon filed for divorce and made arrangements to
move permanently to the chateau, where he planned to spend his
days brooding and drinking good wine.

Dixon's plans were unpleasantly disrupted by the discovery
that the chateau constituted marital property, since it had been
bequeathed to Katie and Dixon together. This meant that Dixon
would either have to sell the chateau and divide the proceeds
with Katie, or give Katie her share of the chateau's value in cash.

Gifts between spouses, unlike gifts from third parties, are *not* considered separate property. If you regularly indulge your spouse in
expensive gifts during your marriage—showering him or her with
jewelry, furs, or expensive electronic equipment—just remember that
all of those gifts will generally count as marital property if you divorce.

One exception to this rule is the engagement ring, which is generally considered the bride's separate property for two reasons. First, the bride usually receives the engagement ring *before* her marriage. Second, engagement rings are conditional gifts, given in exchange for a promise to marry. Once the marriage takes place, the condition is satisfied, and the ring belongs to the bride as her sole property.

EXAMPLE

Cara filed for divorce, assuming that she would be able to afford life on her own by selling some of the jewelry that she had received from Ron over the years. Cara was quite shocked to learn that all of Ron's many gifts to her were not automatically hers to keep. Instead, the gifts constituted marital property and would have to be shared with Ron upon their divorce.

Fortunately for Cara, Ron had presented her with an impressive three-carat engagement ring as a small token of his affection. Cara learned from her lawyer that the engagement ring was hers to keep, free and clear from any marital property claim by Ron.

The moral of the story is that diamonds usually are forever. If an engagement ring is one of your biggest investments, you might want to have a prenuptial agreement in place providing that the engagement ring will be returned to you or will count as marital property in the event of a divorce.

COMPENSATION FOR PERSONAL INJURIES

The rule in many states is that any money you receive as compensation for an injury—such as the settlement from a slip and fall case—is yours to keep in the event of a divorce. However, not too many people are lucky (or unlucky) enough to receive large amounts of money as compensation for personal injuries. But plenty of people end up receiving disability payments at some point in their lives. The law is unclear in many states as to how disability payments are handled. If there is a chance that disability payments might end up being a large chunk of your income while you are married, you might want to look into this issue a bit further.

EXAMPLE

Linda knew that her husband, Bob, would not be able to continue practicing surgery if he suffered even a relatively minor injury to his hands. She encouraged Bob to take out a sizeable disability insurance policy, hoping that this would protect them in the event that Bob was one day unable to practice surgery. Because Linda's lawyer told her that the law in her state was still in flux on the treatment of disability payments in a divorce, Linda also asked Bob to sign a prenuptial agreement, providing that any disability insurance payments would count as marital property in the event of a divorce.

THE APPRECIATION OF SEPARATE PROPERTY

When separate property increases in value during the marriage as a result of market changes or other outside forces, that appreciation is usually also treated as separate property. For example, if the stock you purchased before your marriage increases in value tenfold during your marriage thanks to a breakthrough invention by one of the company's best scientists, the appreciation of your separate property stock will almost certainly be treated as your separate property if you divorce. This is because neither you nor your spouse had anything to do with the increase in value.

The rules are different when separate property increases in value due to the hard work of one or both spouses.

Jordan owned a rather unprofitable delicatessen when he met Katrina, a doe-eyed Russian with a keen business sense. Katrina completely revamped the delicatessen during their marriage. She stocked the shelves with imported biscuits and chocolates, upgraded the cheese selection to include Brie and Camembert, and started offering bread baked fresh from the bakery down the street. Business had nearly tripled by the time Jordan filed for divorce. (He felt Katrina put so much love into her deli sandwiches that there was hardly any love left for him.) Katrina successfully laid claim to the increase in value of Jordan's delicatessen, because his separate property business had appreciated as a direct result of her hard work.

INCOME FROM SEPARATE PROPERTY

When income is earned from separate property during the marriage, that income may or may not be treated as marital property, depending on the state in which you live. Some states do not have a clear rule on this issue. If you or your spouse-to-be will be earning a substantial amount of income from separate property, you might be best served by having an agreement in place specifying how that income will be handled in the event of a divorce.

EXAMPLE

Gabriella had built up a rather impressive stock portfolio before her marriage to Michael. She had focused her investments on companies that paid large dividends, with the hope that her investment income would one day cover all of her living expenses. Michael was a partner in a law firm, miserable with both his hours and his job responsibilities. With Gabriella's encouragement, Michael planned to leave the law to pursue his true passion—acappella singing—after their marriage. Gabriella had run the numbers and assured Michael that her investment income and his savings from slaving away as a lawyer all those years would enable them to live quite comfortably without his partnership profits.

While Michael's heart was in music, Michael's head was still very much focused on the law. He was concerned that if Gabriella divorced him, he would be unable to support himself without a share of her investment income. So he asked Gabriella to sign a prenuptial agreement, providing him with half of all the investment income she earned during their marriage in the event they divorced. (This agreement ensured that Michael would not one day have to sing for his supper.)

THE IMPORTANCE OF KEEPING SEPARATE PROPERTY SEPARATE

To ensure that your separate property will not be divided with your spouse in the event of a divorce, you should be very careful to keep your separate property *entirely separate* from all other property. You should not:

- ◆ change the title of your separate property to joint names (if you own a separate property home, keep that property in your name only);
- ◆ deposit your separate property into a joint account with your spouse; or,
- ◆ use your separate property to pay household or other joint expenses during the marriage. (A divorce court might conclude that by doing so, you treated the separate property as if it were marital property.)

If you mix your separate property with marital property, your separate property may be treated as marital property in the event of a divorce.

EXAMPLE

When Anna and Mason married, they promised that they would share their lives and their love with one another for all eternity. Mason felt that this promise should extend to their finances as well. He promptly changed the title to his four-bedroom home in Georgetown Heights to include Anna's name and deposited all of the savings he had built up before his marriage into their joint account. Mason wanted nothing more than to share his whole world with Anna, including all of his worldly possessions.

Anna was a bit more skeptical of marriage in general. She had seen several of her girlfriends endure nasty divorces, so she wanted to protect herself in the event that the same happened to her. Anna decided to keep all of the money she had earned before they were married in an account in her name only. She never mentioned the existence of this account to Mason and he never asked.

The sad day came when Anna and Mason no longer had anything to talk about. They did not enjoy one another's company anymore and they had drifted apart. In the course of their divorce proceedings, Mason learned for the first time that Anna had a separate savings account, which had grown into a sizeable nest egg. Mason was positively stunned to learn that Anna's savings account was hers to keep, because it was her separate property. All of Mason's premarital property, on the other hand, counted as marital property because Mason—unlike Anna—had failed to keep his separate property separate.

Many couples find that it is unrealistic or even impossible to keep separate property entirely separate during their marriages. The best solution in these cases is to have an agreement in place specifying that separate property will remain separate even if it is kept in joint names during the marriage. You can do this by entering into an agreement that provides that each will retain his or her separate property upon a divorce, free and clear of any claim by the other, regardless of the title in which the property is held during marriage.

The Division of Marital Property

Now that you understand what counts as marital property and what counts as separate property, it is time to turn to the next issue—how marital property is divided in a divorce. A small number of states, such as Nevada, divide marital property equally between spouses at the end of a marriage.

EXAMPLE

> Justin had saved up $40,000 during his five-year marriage to Caitlin. While Justin worked long hours as an architect, often drafting and re-drafting blueprints until late into the night, Caitlin spent her days socializing, shopping, and attending spa appointments. Though Caitlin had contributed very little to their marriage or the family finances, Justin had no choice but to divide his $40,000 equally with Caitlin when they divorced. This is because Justin and Caitlin lived in a state that divides marital property fifty-fifty, regardless of the circumstances of the case.

These *fifty-fifty states* are in the minority. Most states divide marital property equitably, according to what is fair in light of the facts of the case. Courts in these states take into account a number of different factors—known as *equitable distribution factors*—when dividing marital property. The most common equitable distribution factors are:

◆ each spouse's economic and noneconomic contributions to the marriage;

◆ each spouse's contributions to the other's career and earning potential;

◆ each spouse's financial misconduct, if any;

- each spouse's present and future economic circumstances;
- the length of the marriage; and,
- the needs of each spouse, including age and health. (These equitable distribution factors are explained in more detail in the next section.)

In some ways, equitable distribution is far better than the fifty-fifty method because it allows courts to tailor marital property decisions to the unique circumstances of each marriage. This flexibility, however, leads to a great deal of unpredictability. To remedy this drawback of the equitable distribution system, some states will divide marital property equally, unless it would be inequitable to do so in any given case. Couples in these states have a little bit more certainty as to how marital property will be divided. They can each expect to receive half of all marital property unless an equal division would be inappropriate in light of the particular facts of their case.

NOTE: *See Appendix B for a state-by-state summary of divorce distribution laws.*

THE EQUITABLE DISTRIBUTION FACTORS

In states that follow the equitable distribution system, courts will consider the following factors when dividing marital property.

Each spouse's economic and noneconomic contributions to the marriage. Courts will take into account how hard you and your spouse each worked during your marriage and how much you each earned. Courts will also take into account each spouse's noneconomic contributions as a parent and homemaker. Notably, noneconomic contributions to a marriage are often weighted just as heavily as economic contributions.

EXAMPLE

Denise had been a stay-at-home mom while Richard was growing his accounting practice. Denise took care of their four
children, handled all of the household chores, and provided
Richard with an endless supply of support and encouragement. Richard, for his part, turned his fledgling accounting
practice into a booming success during their fifteen-year
marriage. When Denise learned of Richard's relationship with
his secretary, Denise filed for divorce. Richard assumed that
he would get most—if not all—of the property that he had
earned during the marriage. After all, he had been the family
breadwinner while his wife had stayed home. Denise hired the
best lawyer in town and ended up with 60% of the marital
property, much to Richard's astonishment. Denise received a
large share of their marital property because the judge recog-
nized just how hard she had worked to raise their children and
provide Richard with a loving home.

**Each spouse's contributions to the other's career and earning
potential.** If you help to build up your spouse's career—for example,
by working as a nurse so that your spouse can attend medical school or
by moving to a distant state so that your spouse can pursue a lucrative
promotion—courts will take those efforts into account when dividing
marital property. Courts recognize that the spouse who helps to
advance the other spouse's professional life often does so at the
expense of his or her own career.

EXAMPLE

Kyle and Georgia both wanted to go to law school. They knew
that it was financially impossible for both of them to attend law
school at the same time without getting in over their heads in
debt. Because Georgia's LSAT scores were higher, Kyle decided

that Georgia should go to law school first. Kyle worked as a paralegal to pay the household bills, while Georgia burned the midnight oil poring over her law books. After what seemed like an eternity to Kyle, Georgia finally graduated and it was his turn to attend law school. Things were going reasonably well until Georgia announced that she was leaving him. Much to Kyle's shock, Georgia explained that their marriage was getting in the way of her career goals. The only good news is that Kyle did not get the short end of the financial stick in their divorce. He walked away with 75% of the marital property, thanks to the sacrifices he made for Georgia's career.

Each spouse's financial misconduct (if any). If you flagrantly waste marital property during your marriage—for example by buying luxurious gifts for your lover or by gambling away the family's mortgage money—then courts will place great emphasis on that fact when dividing marital property. Courts will not, however, concern themselves if you simply make poor financial decisions or overspend during your marriage.

EXAMPLE

Derek and Melissa fought almost incessantly about money matters from the day they set foot on their honeymoon until the day they decided to file for divorce. Melissa felt that Derek made one financial mistake after the other, first by accepting a low-paying job as an editorial assistant, then by investing some of their money in low-yield bonds, and finally by insisting that they purchase a *fixer-upper* house instead of a small condominium in a thriving neighborhood. Melissa felt that she should end up with more marital property to compensate her for Derek's lack of money smarts. The court disagreed, explaining that since Derek had not actually *wasted* marital property by gambling it away or spending it all on a diamond necklace for his mistress, Derek should not be penalized in their divorce.

The present and future economic circumstances of each spouse. Courts will take into account your separate property, as well as your earning capacity, when dividing marital property.

EXAMPLE

Ted and Meredith had a total of $20,000 in marital property at the end of their eight-year marriage. Because of a downsizing at Ted's company, he had been out of work for over a year. Ted had almost nothing in separate property and no wealthy family members to whom he could turn for support. Meredith, on the other hand, had a $200,000 trust fund. Her father was a wealthy tobacco farmer, who showered her with gifts and spending money on a regular basis. The court awarded Ted 80% of their marital property because Ted really needed the extra funds, while Meredith had more than enough in the way of assets and family support to maintain her lifestyle.

The length of the marriage. The longer the marriage, the more likely a court is to divide marital property equally between a husband and wife. Courts often feel that each spouse's economic and noneconomic contributions tend to even out, more or less, when a couple has been together for a very long time. In short marriages, however, courts tend to emphasize economic contributions over noneconomic contributions.

EXAMPLE

Maria and Samuel had been married for only two years. During this time, Maria had worked as an anchorwoman to pay the family bills while Samuel had taken care of the cooking, cleaning, and other household chores. Because they had no children, Samuel still had most of his day free to play tennis with friends, watch TV, and read mystery novels. At the end of their marriage, the court awarded Maria more than half of their marital property. The court explained that Samuel's noneconomic contributions did not offset Maria's economic contributions since they had been married for such a short time.

The needs of each spouse, including each spouse's age and health. When dividing marital property, courts will take into account the amount that you each need in order to live comfortably. Courts recognize that someone who is old and in poor health probably needs more than a spry 35-year-old who is perfectly capable of supporting him- or herself. Courts also understand that parents of young children often need more in the way of financial support because they might be unable to work full-time due to the needs of their children.

EXAMPLE

Jake and Melanie had been married for five years when Jake filed for divorce. Melanie had given up her career to take care of their two children, Sam and Libby. Though she was once a high-powered corporate lawyer, Melanie now spent her days potty-training Sam (who was two) and chasing Libby (who had just learned to crawl). The court awarded Melanie half of the couple's marital property to enable Melanie to continue devoting her time to Sam and Libby.

THE ROLE OF FAULT IN MARITAL PROPERTY DIVISION

Believe it or not, most states do not take marital fault into account when dividing marital property—regardless of whether your spouse cheats on you, abandons you, or abuses you. This is because courts are increasingly reluctant to delve into the messy details of personal lives when handling the financial aspects of divorce. In a handful of states, however, courts still consider marital fault for the purposes of marital property division. Unfaithful spouses and other misbehaving spouses are often quite heavily penalized and receive disproportionately small shares of marital property in these states. (Check Appendix B to see whether your state takes marital fault into account for the purposes of marital property division.)

Special Categories of Marital Property

Certain categories of marital property merit special mention, because they can be somewhat complicated to value and divide in the event of a divorce. This section addresses the following types of property:

- pensions and other retirement benefits;
- stock options;
- professional licenses and degrees;
- closely held corporations and other businesses; and,
- professional goodwill.

PENSIONS AND OTHER RETIREMENT BENEFITS

You may be surprised to learn that your pension and any other retirement benefits you earn during your marriage will count as marital property. The key question is whether you earn any part of your pension or retirement benefits during your marriage. If so, that portion of your pension or retirement benefits will be divisible with your spouse in the event of a divorce. This is true even if you cannot access your retirement funds or you do not actually receive your pension benefits until many years after your marriage has ended. Moreover, if your pension is unvested at the time you and your spouse divorce and you must work several additional years in order to guarantee your pension, your spouse will still be entitled to his or her share of your pension.

EXAMPLE

Brian was a doorman who had been working in a Park Avenue building for fifteen years. He was married to Heather for ten of those years. The terms of his pension plan required that Brian work for the building for twenty years in order for his pension to vest. Because Brian was married to Heather for ten of the twenty years it would take for his pension to vest, half of his pension benefits constituted marital property.

There are two methods used when dividing a pension or other retirement benefits in the event of a divorce. The first is for the pension holder to *buy out* the other spouse's share of the pension by offering a lump-sum cash payment or by making up the difference with other marital assets. In the previous example, if the marital property share of Brian's retirement amounted to $30,000 (after taking taxes into account), and Brian and Heather agreed that they would divide all marital property in half, Brian could give Heather $15,000 in cash to buy out her share of his retirement.

The second method is for the pension holder to pay the other spouse a share of the pension benefits as and when they are actually paid by using a *qualified domestic relations order* (QDRO). If Heather, from the same example, was entitled to receive half of the marital property share of Brian's pension, which would amount to one quarter of each of Brian's pension checks (since half of Brian's pension constituted marital property). Brian could ask the court for a QDRO. Through a QDRO, Brian and Heather could arrange for 25% of each of Brian's pension checks to be paid directly to Heather by Brian's pension administrator. This would save Brian from having to pay Heather now for pension benefits he would not receive until he retired. A QDRO would also offer Brian the advantage of having Heather be directly responsible for the taxes associated with her share of his pension.

Social Security Benefits. Unlike other types of retirement benefits, Social Security benefits do not count as marital property in the event of a divorce. However, you may be able to receive spousal Social Security benefits based on your spouse's Social Security contributions even after you have divorced, as long as your spouse is eligible for Social Security benefits. Any benefits you receive will not reduce the benefits paid to your former spouse. (Check the Social Security Administration's Web page at **www.ssa.gov** for more information.)

STOCK OPTIONS

Whether you work at a cutting-edge Internet company or a staid blue-chip establishment, there is a good chance that you will receive some part of your compensation in the form of stock options. Stock options are an increasingly common way to reward employees in corporate America. The way stock options generally work is to provide employees with the opportunity to buy or sell the company's stock at a predetermined price (known as the *strike price*) after a certain period of time.

If you are awarded stock options during your marriage, most courts will consider those options to constitute marital property even if you do not actually exercise those options during your marriage. The same holds true if your stock options remain unvested at the time of your divorce and you must remain with the company for a certain number of additional years before you can exercise the options.

You may be wondering why it is that stock options are counted as marital property in the event of a divorce. The reason is that stock options are a form of alternative compensation. If stock options were not a valuable asset in and of themselves, then people would never be willing to accept jobs with lower salaries in exchange for more in the way of stock options, as they so often do.

When stock options are at issue in a divorce, things tend to get a little tricky. The first problem is that it can be difficult to determine what portion of stock options were actually earned during the marriage. This is because stock options are sometimes given as an *incentive* for employees to work hard in the future, and at other times granted as a *thank you* for work well done in the past. Depending on the reason why the stock options were granted, a divorce court might conclude that stock options awarded during the marriage were not actually *earned* during the marriage.

EXAMPLE

Lori received her first set of stock options just six months after she began work at iMagine Group, a multimedia corporation with an Internet-based business model. However, Lori would have to remain with the company for five additional years in order to exercise the options. Lori's husband, Lou, filed for divorce a few weeks after Lori received her first set of stock options. He claimed that the options constituted marital property, since she was awarded the options during her marriage to Lou. Lori argued that the options should not constitute marital property since they were awarded primarily as an incentive for her to work hard for the company for the next five years—all work she would perform *after* her marriage to Lou had ended. The court agreed with Lori, and held that the stock options were her separate property.

However, the exact opposite can happen, depending on the basis for the stock option award.

EXAMPLE

Gary was earning over six figures in the accounting department of a Fortune 500 company when he received unexpected job offers from two competing companies. The first company offered Gary a salary of $200,000, and a signing bonus of $25,000. The second company offered Gary a salary of

$195,000, and a one-time award of 400 stock options, exercisable six months after Gary began work for the company. Gary and his wife agreed that the stock options made the second company's offer much better, even though the annual salary was $5,000 lower.

While Gary enjoyed tremendous career success, his home life was in shambles. Gary and Mia could not conceive a child after years of trying and fertility treatments, and the question of adoption drove the couple apart. Gary did not want to raise a child who was not biologically his own, while Mia wanted more than anything to nurture a child, even if the child had other natural parents.

Mia finally filed for divorce. She claimed that Gary's 400 stock options constituted marital property, since they were granted during the marriage. Gary argued that the stock options should count as his separate property, particularly since he had not exercised even a single option since joining the company. (Gary had no disposable income left after covering the high cost of fertility treatments.) The divorce court agreed with Mia, explaining that Gary's stock options were granted primarily as a signing bonus. The options did not serve as an incentive to perform work in the future, since they were exercisable just six months after Gary joined the company.

To determine whether stock options were in fact earned during the marriage, divorce courts will evaluate whether the options were granted primarily as compensation for past work or as an incentive for future work. Courts will usually consider the following:

- ◆ whether the stock options were offered as a bonus or as an alternative to a fixed salary;
- ◆ whether the value or the quantity of the employee's stock options are tied to future performance;

- whether the plan is used to attract key personnel from other companies; and,
- what the stock option contract specifies with respect to the reason for the granting of the stock options.

Courts often end up concluding that the stock options at issue were earned in part during the marriage and in part after the marriage. Without getting too deep into the details, courts will generally apply a formula of some kind to determine how many of the options constitute marital property. The exact formula used usually depends on the circumstances of the case.

Determining whether stock options constitute marital property—and to what extent—is only half of the battle when dividing stock options in the context of a divorce. Courts must also value the stock options—a very challenging task indeed. The most basic method of valuing stock options is to subtract the strike price from the current trading price.

EXAMPLE

Rob was granted one hundred options to buy his company's stock for $30, at a time when the trading price was $40. A court could determine that each option was worth $10 (the trading price of $40 minus the strike price of $30), and that the total value of his options was $1,000 (one hundred options at $10 each).

A major problem with this simple valuation method is that the stock's trading price could go higher or lower at any point, which would immediately change the value of the options.

The other method for valuing stock options is the *Black-Scholes formula*, which one court has described as *one of the most complicated formulas ever devised*. When attributing a value to stock options, this method takes into account the value and market price of the underlying stock, the exercise price of the options, the volatility of the underlying stock, the amount of time before the option can be exercised, and current interest rates. It usually takes a skilled financial expert even to understand the Black-Scholes formula, let alone apply it to value stock options.

To make matters even more complicated, the mechanics of actually dividing stock options can also be dicey. The first method is for the spouse holding the stock options to buy out the other spouse's share of the options. The problem with this method is that the spouse who holds the options could end up overpaying (or underpaying), because the trading price of the stock at issue could change at any time. If the trading price of the stock at issue changes in value after the date of the divorce, the spouse who holds the options could end up overpaying (or underpaying) the other spouse for his or her share.

Another method is for the spouse who holds the options to divide the options themselves with the other spouse. A husband and wife can simply agree that the nonholder spouse may exercise his or her options at any time after their divorce, simply by providing the spouse who owns the options with the funds necessary to buy (or sell) the stock at issue. The problem with this method is that the spouse holding the options would be liable for all taxes associated with the exercise of the other spouse's options, since stock options are typically nontransferable and nonassignable.

If you or your spouse-to-be is likely to receive any appreciable amount of stock options during your marriage, you would be wise to enter into a prenuptial agreement specifying how those options will be treated in the event of a divorce. Doing so will save you a great deal in the way of time, hassle, and lawyers' fees if the day ever comes when you and your spouse decide to go your separate ways.

PROFESSIONAL LICENSES AND DEGREES

If you earn a professional license or degree during your marriage, then there is a small possibility that a divorce court could consider that license or degree to constitute marital property, subject to division upon divorce. The idea that a professional license or degree could count as marital property might strike you as a bit odd. After all, you cannot sell your professional license or degree for a profit. You cannot hand over your professional license or degree to someone else, and no one else can use it besides you. So how could a license or degree count as property, much less marital property?

To date, New York is the only state whose highest court has determined that licenses and degrees constitute marital property subject to division in a divorce. However, in the future, other states may follow the New York rule and how you handle it could dramatically affect how your property is divided if you divorce. A professional license or degree is sometimes the most valuable asset acquired during the marriage. Treating professional licenses and degrees as marital property provides a means for courts to compensate the spouse who made financial or other sacrifices for the benefit of the professional spouse.

EXAMPLE

Henry was a medical student when he met Camille, a beautiful redhead who earned her living as a nurse in the intensive care unit. Henry was swept away by Camille's bedside manner. The two eloped one crisp fall day, when the smell of apple cider filled the air.

Camille took on extra shifts to help pay the family bills, while Henry spent virtually every waking hour studying medicine. Their cash crunch eased up a bit when Henry began his ophthalmology residency, but Camille still paid for the majority of their household expenses with her growing nursing salary. When Henry was finally ready to begin life as a full-fledged ophthalmologist, Camille was devastated to learn Henry was leaving her. After all her years of hard work, supporting Henry and paying the family bills, Henry was walking out on her just when his salary was about to enter the six-figure range. Livid, Camille called her divorce lawyer and asked him to make sure that Henry paid through the nose to make up for what he had done to her. Fortunately for Camille, the two happened to live in New York, where professional licenses and degrees are counted as marital property.

Camille's lawyer took the case to trial. He presented expert testimony demonstrating that Henry's medical degree and residency training would enable him to earn an average of $185,000 per year, thousands of dollars more than the average college graduate. The expert concluded that the present value of Henry's medical degree and residency training was at least $650,000. Thanks to the hard work of Camille's lawyer, the judge awarded Camille half the value of Henry's medical degree—or $325,000, payable in monthly installments over a five-year period. The judge recognized the sacrifices Camille had made over the years, and wanted to ensure that Camille would be fairly compensated.

Unlike New York, the vast majority of states do not view professional licenses and degrees as marital property. Nevertheless, most divorce courts would not leave Camille empty-handed after her many years of sacrifice. Different states have different ways of compensating the nonprofessional spouse in cases like Camille's.

Some equitable distribution states would simply give Camille a larger share of marital property to make up the difference. Other states would award Camille a healthy amount of spousal support, even though she was perfectly capable of supporting herself through her nursing career. (This type of spousal support is often known as *reimbursement alimony*.) Still other states would only reimburse Camille in the amount of the actual out-of-pocket costs she incurred to support Henry (*e.g.*, tuition bills, costs for books, and so on).

The law with respect to professional licenses and degrees continues to change and evolve. If you plan on earning a license or degree during your marriage, you would be best served by having a prenuptial agreement in place specifying exactly how that license or degree will be handled in the event of a divorce. The same holds true if you expect to be supporting your spouse (whether financially or otherwise) while he or she earns an advanced degree. For example, Camille could have asked Henry to sign a prenuptial agreement providing that in the event of a divorce, she would receive 10% of his earnings for five years if they divorced after he graduated from his ophthalmology residency. A prenuptial agreement provides a vehicle for you and your spouse-to-be to articulate your expectations with respect to contributions to the other's career and earning capacity. Significantly, a prenup can also guarantee the sacrificing spouse some measure of financial protection in the event the marriage fails.

CLOSELY HELD CORPORATIONS AND OTHER BUSINESSES

If you build a business of any kind during your marriage, it generally will be considered marital property in the event of a divorce. The same rule applies if you invest in a closely held corporation during your marriage.

Moreover, if you hold an interest in a business or closely held corporation before your marriage, any increase in value of that business interest that occurs during your marriage will also usually be deemed marital property.

EXAMPLE

Luke owned a hardware store before he married Meg, a woman whose fascination with power tools captured Luke's heart. While Meg did not work at the hardware store alongside her tool-belt sporting husband, Meg helped Luke a great deal with the business in whatever ways she could. Meg often helped Luke select the merchandise, rearranged his store displays, and sent out mailings advertising the latest markdowns on circular saws. If the hardware store appreciated in value during their marriage, Meg would almost certainly be entitled to a share of the appreciation, even though Luke owned the business before his marriage to her.

Businesses and shares of closely held corporations can be quite challenging to value and divide in the context of a divorce. What usually happens is that the spouse who is most closely involved in the business or closely held corporation buys out the other spouse's interest in the business. This means that the business or corporation must first be valued, a task that is much easier said than done. Unlike simple assets, such as cash and shares of publicly traded securities, there is no readily ascertainable value for businesses and closely held corporations. Determining the value of a business or closely held corporation generally requires a sweeping review of the entire business and the expert analysis of a business appraiser or other financial professional. When divorce battles get heated, both spouses usually retain their own valuation experts, and the court may even appoint its own expert. The result is a costly, intrusive, and time-consuming adventure into the finer points of business valuation.

Before a business valuation expert can even begin the process of determining the value of a business, the expert must gather a great deal of information about the business, its operating history, profitability, and prospects for future success. Valuation experts look at a myriad of factors, including:

◆ the nature and history of the business;
◆ the economic outlook in general and the outlook for the specific industry;
◆ the book value of the stock (if any) and the financial condition of the business;
◆ the earning capacity of the company;
◆ the dividend-paying capacity of the company;

- any goodwill value the business has built up; and,
- the market price of actively traded stocks of corporations engaged in the same line of business (for closely held corporations only).

Experts must also review a mountain of financial data and confidential business documents—such as tax returns, detailed profit and loss statements, and the company's balance sheets—before they can begin their analysis.

The fun does not end once an expert has conducted a grueling review of your business operations. The expert must then actually come up with a dollar value for your business using one of several different valuation methods. Unfortunately, the different valuation methods often result in quite different dollar values. As you can imagine, many divorces have taken a turn for the worse when the husband's expert believes the business is worth one amount while the wife's expert assesses the business at a much higher or lower value.

At the risk of boring you with the details, one frequently used valuation method is the *capitalization of earnings method*. An expert using this method will take the business's normal annual earnings and then multiply those earnings by a capitalization factor to arrive at a dollar value for the business. Small businesses are usually valued at a capitalization rate of somewhere between one and four times net earnings.

EXAMPLE

Vera had a bridal boutique that averaged about $125,000 in net profits each year. When Vera filed for divorce from her husband, Tom, a man whose potbelly had grown so large that he had not seen his feet in months, asked for a share of her business. Vera and Tom appointed a mutually agreed-upon valuation expert who used the capitalization of earnings method to value her bridal boutique. The expert concluded that an appropriate capitalization rate would be twice the net earnings. This meant that Vera's bridal boutique was valued at $250,000 (her net annual profits of $125,000 x 2).

When a business or closely held corporation is at issue, most divorces do not proceed quite as neatly as Vera's case. Both spouses often end up spending substantial sums of money on expert fees and legal bills, not to mention a great deal of time. If either you or your spouse-to-be now owns or expects to invest in a business or closely held corporation, you would probably be best served by having a prenuptial agreement in place specifying how your business will be valued and divided in the event of a divorce.

EXAMPLE

Jenny's soon-to-be-husband, Howard, owned a profitable fruit and vegetable store in Madison, Wisconsin. Jenny expected to work side-by-side with Howard during their marriage, to ensure the continued success of the store. While Jenny loved Howard with all of her heart, she was worried about what would happen if she and Howard divorced at some point in the future. After all, the fruit and vegetable store would probably be the largest asset in the marriage. Jenny decided to ask Howard to spell out her rights in advance, in a prenuptial agreement. Jenny and Howard agreed that if they decided to part ways, Jenny would receive 15% of the grocery store's gross receipts for five years following the divorce. This way, Jenny would be compensated for her hard work, but neither Jenny nor Howard would have to engage in the costly process of valuing the fruit and vegetable store.

PROFESSIONAL GOODWILL

If you are a professional in private practice or you plan to start a professional practice during your marriage, you should be aware that the *goodwill* (reputation) value of your practice could be subject to division in the event of a divorce. Professional practices are different than other businesses because the only real business asset of any value is the practice's reputation and prestige. If a professional practice would yield a very low value using traditional business valuation methods, courts will consider taking into account the practice's reputation value to ensure that the other spouse does not end up walking away from the marriage empty-handed.

The notion that your professional reputation could be divided in a divorce probably strikes you as mind-boggling. After all, a reputation is not the kind of asset that you can deposit in a bank. But consider this—professional practices are often sold for considerable sums even when the only assets of any value are the waiting room chairs and the patient/client files. Why are buyers willing to pay for businesses with virtually nothing in the way of tangible assets? Because the goodwill value of the business ensures that the business will be profitable in the future.

Depending on the circumstances of your case and the state in which you live, the goodwill value of your professional practice may or may not be considered marital property. If a court decides that your professional goodwill is up for grabs in the event of a divorce, it may be valued using the *capitalization of excess earnings method*. This method compares your earnings to the earnings of an average professional in your field and geographical area, with experience, expertise, and education similar to your own. Your *excess earnings* (your actual earnings minus the average earnings of a similarly situated professional) would then be multiplied by a capitalization factor to arrive at a value for your professional goodwill.

EXAMPLE

William was a very successful psychotherapist who regularly counseled the rich and famous, including several prominent movie stars and one manic-depressive heiress. William earned approximately a million dollars a year, nearly four times what the average psychotherapist in his area and with his credentials was bringing home each year. When William's wife, Polly, filed for divorce, she demanded a share of William's professional goodwill. An expert appointed by the court concluded that William's *excess earnings* amounted to $750,000 (William's earnings minus the earnings of an average psychotherapist in his area) and that an appropriate capitalization factor would be 100% (or one times earnings). William's professional goodwill would therefore be worth $750,000, and Polly would be entitled to quite a pretty penny in their divorce.

If you are a professional with a promising career, you would be well-served by having a prenuptial agreement in place specifying exactly how your professional goodwill will be handled in the event of a divorce. Some people mistakenly believe that they do not need a prenuptial agreement because the partnership agreements for their professional practices (often known as *buy-sell agreements*) already set forth a value for the practice's professional goodwill. This is dangerous because courts do not automatically accept the goodwill values set forth in partnership agreements when making decisions in a divorce. Your partnership agreement might provide that your practice's goodwill is worth zero, for example, so the partnership will have to pay as little as possible if one partner decides to leave the practice. A divorce court, however, might still decide that your practice's goodwill is worth several hundred thousand dollars, despite the provisions of your partnership agreement.

Spousal Support

Unlike unmarried lovers, who are usually not considered to owe one other anything in the eyes of the law, husbands and wives have a financial obligation to support one another. This financial obligation can continue even after the relationship has ended. If one spouse lacks the funds to provide for his or her own reasonable needs after a divorce, the other spouse may have to provide regular economic support until the financially dependent spouse can cover his or her own expenses. These spousal support payments are often referred to as *alimony* or *maintenance*.

Once upon a time, only husbands paid alimony to wives—never the other way around. Wives were almost always guaranteed some amount of support in the event of a divorce. These support payments often continued for years and years. Things have changed a great deal since then. Women may now be required to support their former husbands if the economic circumstances warrant. Moreover, spousal support is no longer the *sure thing* that it once was. Courts award spousal support in only a fraction of divorce cases. When spousal support is granted, courts usually place limits on the amount and duration of support. The new thinking in the courtrooms is that people should not have to provide for their former spouses for the rest of their lives. Courts now tend to believe that each spouse should provide for his or her own needs after a divorce (or at least soon thereafter).

FACTORS CONSIDERED IN AWARDING SPOUSAL SUPPORT

Most states do not have any precise guidelines in place specifying how much spousal support will be awarded, or for how long, in the event of a divorce. Judges generally have complete control over spousal support decisions and can resolve the issue of spousal support in any way they see fit. When determining whether to order one spouse to support the other, judges will consider the following.

The present and future financial circumstances of each spouse. The key inquiry for the purposes of alimony is whether one spouse has enough assets and income to provide for his or her own reasonable needs. Support decisions are made in conjunction with marital property division decisions. If one spouse receives a large share of marital property, for example, then a court might consider it unnecessary to award that spouse alimony.

The earning capacity of the spouse seeking support. A significant factor with respect to spousal support is whether the spouse seeking financial assistance has enough education and experience to find reasonably lucrative employment. Courts will usually (but not always) take a realistic view of each spouse's ability to support him- or herself. When one spouse has been out of the workforce for many years, engaged in the full-time tasks of homemaking or raising a family, courts will generally recognize that such an individual will require substantial economic help in order to become self-supporting. Courts will sometimes even require one spouse to support the other indefinitely in such cases.

The reasonable needs of the spouse seeking support. When determining whether the financially dependent spouse can provide for his or her own reasonable needs, courts factor in the lifestyle the couple enjoyed during their marriage. The pampered husband of a wealthy distant cousin of the British royal family, for example, would be considered to have different *reasonable needs* than the frugal wife of a grocery store clerk. Courts will also take into account one spouse's need to work fewer hours, or to stay at home full-time, in order to take care of young children.

The length of the marriage. Courts place great emphasis on the length of the marriage when considering the issue of spousal support. A court is much more likely to award spousal support in a long marriage of twenty years than in a short marriage of three to five years.

The support-seeking spouse's contributions to the other spouse's career and earning potential. When one spouse has made economic or career sacrifices in order to advance the other spouse's career, courts often use spousal support as a means of compensating the sacrificing spouse. This type of spousal support is sometimes referred to as *reimbursement alimony*. Depending on the state, reimbursement alimony may be limited to the actual economic contributions (such as tuition payments) one spouse made to the other spouse's career or earning capacity.

The support-seeking spouse's economic and noneconomic contributions to the marriage. Courts will take into account the support-seeking spouse's efforts as a parent and homemaker when awarding spousal support. For example, if one spouse made significant career sacrifices for the sake of the family, then a court would be inclined to award alimony to help that spouse get back on his or her feet.

Fault. Most states do not consider marital fault when deciding whether or not to grant spousal support. Though it may seem unfair, most states would still require you to support a financially dependent spouse even if he or she cheated on you or abandoned you. However, a small number of states—such as Texas—will factor in marital fault when determining spousal support. In these states, a spouse who is guilty of adultery or other types of marital fault may be precluded from receiving support regardless of the financial circumstances of the case.

ENDING SPOUSAL SUPPORT

Spousal support usually ends the moment that the support-paying spouse dies, even if there are several years of scheduled support payments remaining.

Diana was awarded four thousand dollars a month in support after her marriage to Philip, a wealthy hedge fund manager, ended in divorce. Diana's support payments were supposed to continue for five years. Unfortunately for Diana, Philip paid more attention to his bank balance than his cholesterol. His regular diet of Argentinian steaks and Cuban cigars finally got the better of him, and he died just three months after his divorce was finalized. Diana was devastated to learn that her support payments had suffered the same fate as Philip, even though Philip had left behind an estate worth several million dollars.

Spousal support also generally ends when the financially dependent spouse remarries. Some states even terminate spousal support payments when the financially dependent spouse begins living with someone else in a marriage-like relationship.

TAXES

Spousal support is normally taxable to the recipient and tax-deductible to the payer. In other words, the financially dependent spouse has to pay taxes on every dollar of spousal support received. This usually takes a big chunk out of each month's support check. It is not a requirement that spousal support be taxable to the recipient. Either in a prenuptial agreement or as part of a divorce settlement agreement, a couple can agree that the financially dependent spouse will receive all spousal support payments entirely tax free. If spousal support is not taxable to the recipient, however, the spouse paying support cannot deduct the support payments for tax purposes.

3

Till Death Do Us Part: Prenups and Estate Planning

Few things are as unpleasant to contemplate as your own death or the death of a loved one. When marriage is on the horizon, however, it is extremely important that you consider what will happen in the event that you or your spouse-to-be dies unexpectedly. Because spouses have certain automatic rights to one another's estates, your assets might end up being distributed after your death in a way that you never would have intended.

This chapter begins by providing a general overview of what happens to property when someone dies. It then explains how your assets will be distributed if you die without a will and what portion of your estate your spouse-to-be will be entitled to inherit simply by virtue of your upcoming marriage. This chapter also discusses ways to ensure that you and your spouse-to-be will both be adequately provided for in case one of you dies prematurely. Hopefully you will be blessed with the privilege of growing old and gray with your spouse. If tragedy strikes before then, however, you will be much better off if you took the time to plan for the worst (all the while hoping for the best).

An Overview of Estate Law

You might be surprised to learn that not all property gets distributed according to the terms of a will. Many categories of property—such as funds held in joint accounts and retirement savings plans—are transferred directly to the joint owner or the *beneficiary* (the person designated by the owner as the recipient of the property in the event of his or her death) when someone dies. Because the process of settling a will (known as *probate*) can be time-consuming and costly, many people try to arrange their affairs so that as much property as possible passes directly to the intended recipient outside of probate.

PROPERTY HELD IN JOINT TENANCY

If you own property together with someone in the form of a *joint tenancy with rights of survivorship*, that property will automatically go to your co-owner in the event of your death. Married couples often hold bank accounts, brokerage accounts, and own real estate as joint tenants with rights of survivorship. These assets go directly to the surviving spouse when one spouse passes away. They also pass free and clear of any claim by others, such as children from a first marriage.

RETIREMENT BENEFITS

Most retirement plans—such as 401(k) accounts and individual retirement accounts (IRAs)—allow you to designate a beneficiary to whom your retirement savings or other retirement benefits will go in the event of your death. Since retirement benefits can amount to a substantial part of a person's total asset base, the law provides that you must designate your spouse as the beneficiary of most retirement plans. You will generally need your spouse's written consent in order to designate someone else as the beneficiary of these retirement plans.

EXAMPLE

Carla listed her daughter, Gloria, as the beneficiary of each of her retirement accounts. When Carla married Felix, her benefits administrator informed Carla that she would either have to change the beneficiary designation to Felix or ask Felix to sign a written waiver allowing her to name Gloria as the beneficiary of these plans. Fortunately for Carla, Felix was more than happy to sign whatever was necessary to enable Gloria to remain as the named beneficiary of Carla's retirement accounts. He knew that Gloria's father had abandoned her when she was very young. He wanted to ensure that Gloria would be well provided for in the event of her mother's death.

LIFE INSURANCE PROCEEDS

Like retirement benefits, life insurance proceeds are paid directly to a named beneficiary in the event of the insured's death. As you probably already know, a life insurance policy is a contract between you and an insurance company, pursuant to which the insurance company must pay a certain amount of money to your designated beneficiary in the event of your death. You do not need to name your spouse as the beneficiary of your life insurance policy. Rather, you can choose anyone you want—even a charity or nonprofit organization—as the beneficiary of your life insurance proceeds.

EXAMPLE

Simon purchased a $500,000 term life insurance policy and designated his aging parents as the beneficiaries so they would have enough funds to pay for health care and nursing home costs in the event of his death. Simon also had a very small cattle ranch in New Mexico and a vintage bottle cap collection worth a little more than a thousand dollars. When Simon suffered a fatal blow to the head, his wife, Maureen, received only the cattle ranch and the bottle cap collection pursuant to the terms of Simon's will. The most substantial asset—the life insurance proceeds—passed to Simon's parents outside of Simon's will.

PROPERTY WITH A PAY-ON-DEATH DESIGNATION OR BENEFICIARY DEED

Property with a *pay-on-death (POD)* or *transfer-on-death (TOD)* designation also goes directly to the named beneficiary in the event of the owner's death. In some states, *beneficiary deeds* accomplish the same purpose. These options allow people to enjoy the convenience of a *joint tenancy* (which allows property to pass directly to the co-owner of the property in the event of one's death) without giving up control of the property during their lifetimes.

EXAMPLE

Aaron wanted his sister, Danielle, to have whatever was left in his checking account when he died. He wanted to avoid probate and ensure that Danielle would have access to the funds as soon as possible after his death. However, Aaron was nervous about holding his checking account jointly with Danielle during his lifetime, because she was a bit of a spendthrift. If Danielle were a joint tenant on the account, she would have the same privileges to withdraw money or write checks on the account as Aaron. So Aaron set up a *pay-on-death* designation, providing that the funds in his checking account would go directly to Danielle when he died. This allowed him to maintain control of the account while he was alive, but also have the funds transferred directly to Danielle in the event of his death.

PROPERTY HELD IN TRUST

Particularly when people have accumulated a sizeable amount of wealth, they often put some or all of their property into trust for estate planning or other purposes. Property held in trust is handed down directly to the trust's beneficiary (or beneficiaries) in accordance with the terms of a trust.

EXAMPLE

Arthur had always wanted to leave the bulk of his estate to his alma mater, Columbia University. After talking with his tax and estate law attorneys, Arthur decided to put his stock portfolio into a charitable trust. The trust paid him the stock dividends during his lifetime, but provided that the stocks themselves would be turned over to Columbia University when he died. Arthur's wife, Lucille, paid no attention when Arthur explained why he was setting up the trust and how the trust would work. (Arthur had a habit of explaining even the simplest things in excruciating detail, and Lucille had managed to survive their conversations only by tuning him out for long stretches at a time.) It was not until Arthur died that Lucille realized (much to her shock) that the bulk of Arthur's assets had long since been gifted to Columbia University, pursuant to a living trust.

ℰ℠ ℰ℠ ℰ℠

With the exception of the categories of property just discussed, the other property you own at the time of your death will be distributed pursuant to the terms of your will. If you do not have a will, the property in your estate will be allocated according to your state's laws of *intestate succession.* However, regardless of whether or not you leave behind a will, *your spouse has certain automatic property rights to your estate simply by virtue of having married you.* These property rights are discussed in the next two sections.

Dying Without a Will

If you or your spouse dies without leaving behind a will, your property will be distributed according to the default rules of *intestate succession*. Different states have dramatically different rules for intestate succession. However, all states presume that you would want to leave a sizeable portion of your estate to your surviving spouse. In some states, your entire estate goes to your surviving spouse if you have no children when you die.

The intestate succession rules also make certain assumptions about how much of your estate you would want to leave to your parents or your children. Most states will reduce your surviving spouse's share of your estate if you leave children behind. Some states will also reduce your surviving spouse's share if your parents are still alive when you die. Significantly, no state's intestate succession rules will take your friends, extended family members, stepfamily members, or desires to contribute towards charitable causes into account when dividing and distributing your estate.

In some cases, the intestate succession rules work reasonably well.

EXAMPLE

Fred never got around to meeting with a lawyer and writing a will (even though his wife, Maggie, reminded him at least once a month to do so). Fred did not have too much in the way of assets—only a house he owned with Maggie, a couple of old Hondas, and a few thousand dollars in the bank. He and Maggie had never had children and Fred's parents had died years ago. Unfortunately for both Fred and Maggie, Fred made the fatal mistake of dozing off while operating some heavy equipment on a construction site one day. The intestate succession laws of Fred's state provided that his entire estate went to Maggie—which is exactly what Fred would have wanted.

Not all cases are as straightforward as Fred and Maggie's. Look at some other examples in which the rules of intestate succession did not have the desired outcome.

EXAMPLE 1

Cynthia had long-since stopped speaking to her father, who had never accepted her husband, Evan, because of his biracial lineage. When Cynthia died without a will, Evan was stunned to learn he would have to share Cynthia's estate with her estranged father under the intestate succession laws of their state. Had Cynthia realized this, she would have been certain to draft a will cutting her father out of her estate and leaving everything to her dearest Evan.

EXAMPLE 2

Ralph was fatally bitten by a shark just days after he and Sasha began their Hawaiian honeymoon. Ralph had been supporting his senile mother for years and had planned to continue helping her throughout her old age. Unfortunately for Ralph's mother, Ralph died without leaving behind a will making his intentions clear. The intestate succession laws of his state provided that all of his property went to Sasha, his wife of three days, and his mother received nothing. Had Ralph known of this possibility, he would have been certain to draft a will providing generously for Mama.

EXAMPLE 3

After two rather bad marriages, Perry finally found true love and contentment with Genevieve, a French-bred woman with a fondness for terriers and truffles. Perry had three grown children, all of whom were millionaires in their own right. (Perry's first wife had been a baroness.) Genevieve, however, had virtually no assets of any kind. When Perry took a fatal misstep while climbing Mount Everest, Genevieve learned for the first time that Perry had forgotten to draft a will. Under the laws of their state, Genevieve received only one-third of Perry's modest estate while Perry's grown children (who had no need for Perry's money) received the remainder. Had Perry spent more time focusing on his finances and less time scaling perilous mountains, he would have drafted a will leaving his heart, soul, and bank accounts to his true love, Genevieve.

To ensure that your state's government does not make these important estate-related decisions for you, take the time to plan your estate and draft a will that clearly states what you would like to have happen to your assets when you die. You should also make sure that your soon-to-be spouse does the same, so that all of your property is ultimately allocated exactly as you each intend.

If you already have a will, give some serious thought to amending it or rewriting it now that a new marriage is on the horizon. Why? Because in some states, a will made prior to marriage is considered null and void after your marriage has taken place if it does not explicitly reference your upcoming marriage. The purpose of this is to ensure that people do not accidentally disinherit their spouses by forgetting to update their wills after their marriages.

When Your Spouse Can Rewrite Your Will

While single folks are free to will their property to whomever they please, married people do not have this privilege. The law in every state essentially requires that you leave a certain portion of your estate—known as the *elective share*—to your surviving spouse. In most states, the elective share is one-third to one-half of your estate. If you fail to leave at least this amount to your spouse in your will, your spouse has the right to elect against your will and claim an elective share of your estate. In other words, your spouse is entitled to inherit a significant portion of your estate regardless of the provisions of your will. Depending on the state in which you live, your spouse might also have the right to keep the home you both lived in when you were alive.

As is the case with the rules of intestate succession, the elective share rules make perfect sense in some cases.

EXAMPLE

Troy and Heidi were married for twenty years, and had three children together. Heidi was almost completely financially dependent on Troy and had devoted her life to their marriage and children. Unbeknownst to Heidi, Troy had been engaging in a number of extramarital trysts and had become quite attached to one lover in particular. Troy had also prepared a do-it-yourself will pursuant to which left his entire estate to Cecilia, the long-legged waitress who had become his favorite companion. When Troy was fatally hit in the head one day with a foul ball at the ballpark, Heidi was beside herself with grief—until she read Troy's will. Fuming, Heidi hired the best lawyer in town and claimed her elective share in the amount of half of Troy's estate. Had it not been for the elective share rules, Heidi would have been left destitute by Troy's heartless will.

While the elective share rules serve a useful purpose in some cases, the rules lead to illogical results in other cases.

EXAMPLE

It took Larry almost ten years to get over the death of his first wife, Violet. After much prodding, Larry finally made his way out into the singles scene again and met and married Celeste, a noted architect. Larry's four daughters were all part of the wedding party and each gave her blessing for Larry to move on with his life. When Larry died, he left five percent of his estate to Celeste, who was more than capable of supporting herself, and the remainder of his estate to his four girls. Much to the shock of Larry's daughters, Celeste elected against Larry's will and claimed one-third of his entire estate. This left much less for Larry's daughters, all of whom were just starting out and badly needed their inheritance funds to make their way in the world. Had Larry thought that Celeste would claim her elective share of his estate, he would have heeded his lawyer's advice and asked Celeste to sign a prenuptial agreement waiving her elective share rights.

As if all of this is not complicated enough already, the elective share rules also vary a great deal from state to state. In many states, the surviving spouse is entitled to an elective share in the amount of one-third or one-half of the deceased spouse's estate. In a few states, the surviving spouse is only entitled to one-half of the property earned during the marriage. In a handful of other states, the surviving spouse is entitled to a sliding scale percentage of the deceased spouse's estate—which can be less than 3% in a short marriage.

Moreover, what counts as the deceased spouse's *estate* for purposes of the elective share is different in different states. For example, in some states, property held in trust counts as part of the deceased spouse's estate for purposes of the elective share, even though that property passes outside of the probate process. These variations mean that your inheritance rights as a spouse can change dramatically if you do something as simple as moving across the border to the state next door.

ॐ ॐ ॐ

If you plan to leave a sizeable amount of your property to someone other than your spouse, you should be very careful to ensure that the elective share rules do not frustrate your plans. In addition, you should seriously consider asking your spouse to sign a prenuptial agreement waiving his or her right to an elective share of your estate.

You should also be certain to familiarize yourself with the elective share rules if you would be unable to support yourself at a comfortable level without your spouse's financial assistance. Depending on your state's elective share rules, you might not be adequately protected if your spouse fails to leave you with sufficient assets in his or her will. Instead of relying on the elective share rules to ensure that you receive a fair share of your spouse's estate, the better course of action is to ask your spouse to agree in advance to leave you a certain amount of his or her estate. For example, your prenuptial agreement could provide that you are entitled to at least one half of your deceased spouse's estate, regardless of the terms of your spouse's will or the elective share laws of your state.

Life Insurance

As you and your spouse-to-be begin the process of estate planning, you should assess whether you would both be able to support yourselves comfortably if one of you died prematurely. If either one of you would suffer financially in the event of the other's death, you should give some serious thought to purchasing life insurance.

There are two basic types of life insurance—term life insurance and permanent life insurance. *Term life insurance* only insures you for a certain period of time (for example, fifteen years). Once that period of time is over, a term life insurance policy has no value whatsoever and pays no benefits upon your death. *Permanent life insurance*, on the other hand, pays benefits regardless of when you die and also accrues a cash value as you pay premiums over time. Because of these differences, term life insurance is generally much less expensive.

When it comes to buying life insurance, time is money. Both term and permanent life insurance policies cost much less for people who are young and healthy than for older people suffering from a health condition of any kind. If you or your spouse-to-be expect to buy life insurance at some point, you should do so sooner rather than later to obtain the most favorable rates.

QTIP Trusts

Depending on your circumstances, you may be facing the competing estate planning goals of providing adequately for your surviving spouse while ensuring that the bulk of your assets go to your children from a prior marriage, your favorite charity, or some other beneficiary. A *QTIP trust* is one way to solve this problem. Short for *qualified terminable interest property trust*, a QTIP trust allows you to leave your assets to your surviving spouse for the duration of his or her lifetime. When your surviving spouse dies, the assets in the QTIP trust then get passed on to your children or grandchildren from a prior marriage, or anyone else whom you wish to designate as the beneficiary. Using a device such as QTIP trust enables you to leave a sizeable amount of your estate to your spouse without losing control over the ultimate disposition of the property. A QTIP trust also allows you to take advantage of the powerful *marital deduction,* which provides that an inheritance one spouse receives from the other is entirely exempt from estate taxes.

A QTIP trust can be complicated and is not for everyone. In some estate-planning situations, however, a QTIP trust is an elegant and sensible solution.

EXAMPLE

Both Gordon and Emily had been married before and had children of their own when they met and married during a bicycling tour in Ireland. While Emily had very little in the way of assets, Gordon had built up an estate worth hundreds of thousands of dollars thanks to the success of his New Orleans restaurant and his cooking show syndication. Gordon wanted to leave as much of his estate as possible to Emily, since she was his soulmate and best friend. However, Gordon was concerned that Emily would then leave these assets to her own children—rather than his children—when she died. While Gordon cared a great deal for Emily's children, he felt very strongly that his assets should ultimately go to his own children and grandchildren. So Gordon worked with his lawyer to set up a QTIP trust, providing that Emily would be entitled to the income from his assets (and the principal, if necessary) to cover her reasonable living expenses during her lifetime. Once Emily died, the assets in the trust would then go directly to Gordon's children and grandchildren. In essence, the QTIP trust ensured that Emily could not affect the ultimate disposition of Gordon's assets through her own will.

If you are in a predicament similar to Gordon's, talk to a trusts and estates lawyer about setting up a QTIP trust or otherwise structuring your estate to achieve your competing goals of providing for your surviving spouse while retaining control over the final disposition of your assets.

Writing Your Own Vows: The Prenuptial Agreement

Now that you understand the default rules that govern marriages when it comes to debt, divorce, and death, it is time to consider a powerful alternative to these rules—the prenuptial agreement. Prenuptial agreements allow couples to write their own vows, so to speak. If you choose to enter into a prenuptial agreement, you and your spouse will be able to decide for yourselves how your property will be allocated in the event of death or divorce. You can also specify who will have responsibility for your various debts and under what circumstances. You can even use your prenuptial agreement as a tool for establishing how you will manage your money during your marriage.

Prenuptial agreements are probably not be for everyone. Some people feel that prenuptial agreements destroy the romance by forcing lovers to focus on the unpleasant practicalities of married life instead of sharing rosy visions for their life together. Others believe that prenups get marriages off on the wrong foot, because couples end up planning for the worst instead of the best. Whatever the drawbacks of prenuptial agreements, however, the experts agree that prenuptial agreements make good financial and practical sense. One state's highest court neatly summed up the benefits of prenups as follows.

Prenuptial agreements...provide...people with the opportunity to ensure pre-dictability, plan their future with more security and, most importantly, decide their own destiny. Moreover, allowing couples to think through the financial aspects of their marriage beforehand can only foster strength and permanency in [their] relationship[s].

Brooks v. Brooks, 733 P.2d 1044, 1050 (Alaska 1987).

This chapter will empower you to make an educated decision on whether or not a prenuptial agreement is right for you. First, you are introduced to the advantages and disadvantages of prenuptial agreements. Then there is an explanation why certain categories of people—such as individuals with children from a prior marriage—should strongly consider entering into a prenuptial agreement or taking other measures to protect themselves and those they love.

The Upsides of Prenups

At the risk of sounding like a paid advertisement from the prenup lobby, the advantages of prenuptial agreements are almost too numerous to list. The following are four of the most important upsides of entering into a prenup.

A prenup provides you with valuable insight into your soon-to-be spouse's personal finances. Sometimes, lovers who share even their innermost thoughts with one another cannot bring themselves to share their bank statements or other personal financial details. Entering into a prenuptial agreement forces soon-to-be newlyweds to share this information with one another, because full financial disclosure is an integral part of the prenup process. Having a thorough understanding of one another's income, assets, and liabilities will enable you and your spouse to make far better financial decisions in your marriage.

EXAMPLE

Julia and Mark had talked about everything in the world—or so it seemed—before Mark proposed under a canopy of stars in Grand Canyon National Park. Julia had agreed that she would leave her job as a human resources director in Illinois and move to Nashville, where Mark planned to take over the reins of his father's manufacturing plant. When she made this decision, Julia had no idea that the profits at the manufacturing plant were declining each year and that the company was proceeding in the direction of bankruptcy. And Mark had no idea that while Julia earned about fifty thousand dollars per year, the stock options, retirement, and other benefits she received brought her total annual income up to over a hundred and fifty thousand dollars. Had Mark and Julia taken the time to provide each other with complete details of their financial situations, as is required when negotiating a prenuptial agreement, the couple would have soon realized that they would be able to earn much more if Julia kept her job and the couple stayed in Illinois.

The process of negotiating a prenuptial agreement provides a healthy springboard for having your important money management discussions before you tie the knot. Believe it or not, married couples fight more about money than any other issue. Money even trumps in-laws as the number one cause of arguments between husbands and wives. So what's the solution? Hammering out your money differences *before* you walk down the aisle, through a prenuptial agreement. While it would be next to impossible to anticipate and avoid all of your future money-related arguments, discussing financial issues in advance of your marriage will almost certainly help you and your spouse understand where you agree and disagree when it comes to money matters.

Jeremy and Natasha thought that their main differences lay in their fashion sensibilities—Jeremy had none, and was perfectly content to build his entire wardrobe from whatever was on sale at the Gap. Natasha was a true fashionista who, to the utter confusion of her friends, loved Jeremy despite his frumpiness. What Natasha and Jeremy did not realize was that their fashion differences paled in comparison to their money-related differences. Natasha thought nothing of spending several hundred dollars on a pair of shoes, while Jeremy agonized over purchasing even a pair of socks if it was not on sale.

Fortunately for both of them, Natasha had suggested that she and Jeremy enter into a prenuptial agreement, which required that she and Jeremy exchange the intimate details of their personal finances. Jeremy balked when he saw Natasha's monthly credit card bills, and Natasha was shocked to see just how little of his income Jeremy actually spent each month. They both quickly realized that a system in which they completely merged their finances during their marriage would not work for either of them. Jeremy would be unable to bear the stress of Natasha's reckless spending and Natasha would soon resent Jeremy if he constantly badgered her about her shopping habits. So Jeremy and Natasha agreed that they would each deposit a certain amount of their income into a joint account to cover rent and other shared expenses. The rest of their income, as well as their debt, would remain entirely separate.

A prenuptial agreement can protect your assets and save you thousands of dollars in legal fees—in case life does not turn out exactly as you have planned. Instead of leaving it up to the divorce laws of your state to decide what counts as marital property and what counts as separate property, you can use a prenuptial agreement to define what property will be divided—and what property will remain yours and yours alone—in the event your marriage ends in divorce.

A prenuptial agreement allows you to write your own rules for your marriage, instead of letting the government do it for you. The default marriage rules strike many people as illogical. Why is it that everything you earn during your marriage counts as marital property? How come your spouse is entitled to an automatic share of everything in your estate, even if your will says otherwise? Why is it that there is no formula in place for calculating spousal support? A prenuptial agreement can liberate you from the rules that you do not like and empower you to decide for yourself what terms will govern your marriage. More importantly, a prenuptial agreement can ensure that your life will not change even if the laws do.

EXAMPLE

Edward was a lonely divorcé with two young children when he met Marianna. Marianna was a vivacious ice skater with a quick wit and a hearty laugh. Edward fell in love with Marianna without even realizing it. Soon the two were planning their honeymoon in Greece.

While Edward was eagerly looking forward to married life with Marianna, he was nervous about the consequences of marriage when it came to his property rights. He thought it was absurd that Marianna would be entitled to a share of his estate even if his will provided otherwise. So he asked Marianna to enter into a prenuptial agreement, agreeing that *all* of his property would go to his two children in the event of his death. Marianna understood that Edward wanted to make sure that his children would be protected if he died prematurely, but she explained to Edward that she, too, deserved some protection, especially if she ended up foregoing a position with the Ice Capades to help him care for his children.

So what was the solution? In exchange for Marianna's waiving her right to an elective share of Edward's estate, Edward agreed to purchase a five hundred thousand dollar life insurance policy naming Marianna as the beneficiary. This way, Edward's children and Marianna would both be provided for in the event of Edward's death. A prenuptial agreement allowed Edward and Marianna to craft the rules that would make sense in their marriage, instead of simply signing on to the default *one-size-fits-all* marriage rules.

The Downsides of Prenups

While just about every financial planner will tell you that a prenuptial agreement is a good idea, you should be aware that there are some potential downsides to entering into one.

You could strike a bad deal in your prenuptial agreement. Particularly if your spouse-to-be is significantly wealthier than you, there is a risk that your prenuptial agreement could be dramatically lopsided in favor of him or her. It is certainly appropriate for you to agree that certain categories of your soon-to-be spouse's property will remain off-limits in the event of a divorce. If your soon-to-be spouse asks you to sign a prenup that effectively waives all your property rights and rights to support in the event of a divorce, however, you have reason to be concerned. A prenup should never be a one-sided document, even if one spouse-to-be is the heir to the throne of a small European country while the other is a penniless pauper.

Sometimes the less well-off spouse-to-be feels compelled to sign almost any agreement presented by the other, as if to prove that he or she truly is marrying for love and not money. *Do not make this mistake.* A prenuptial agreement is by no means a sign of your commitment and devotion to your spouse-to-be. In fact, if he or she wants you to sign away basically all your property rights in the event of a divorce, you should seriously question his or her commitment and devotion to you.

EXAMPLE

Dimitri asked Courtney whether she would sign a prenuptial agreement before he had even popped the question. The son of an oil baron, Dimitri was worth over a hundred million dollars. The prenuptial agreement Dimitri proposed provided that Courtney would not be entitled to any of his assets or any alimony in the event of a divorce. Courtney balked when she saw the agreement. The prenup would leave her with absolutely nothing even if she remained married to Dimitri for twenty-five years. Courtney explained to Dimitri that the agreement was incredibly unfair and that she would only sign a prenuptial agreement that provided her with some protection in the event of a divorce.

Courtney's lawyer negotiated with Dimitri's lawyer for a few weeks and a suitable agreement was soon reached. The final prenup provided that all of Dimitri's assets would remain his separate property in the event of a divorce, and that Courtney would receive no alimony, exactly as Dimitri had initially suggested. However, the prenup also provided that for every year the couple remained married, Dimitri would contribute two hundred thousand dollars to an investment account in Courtney's sole name. The funds in the investment account would be Courtney's to keep, free and clear, in the event of a divorce.

The investment account insured that Courtney would not suffer a tremendous decline in her standard of living after a divorce and made Courtney confident that she could walk away from her career without losing her ability to support herself. Both Courtney and Dimitri were comfortable with the terms of the revised prenuptial agreement.

The moral of the story is that even if your spouse-to-be is much richer than you are, you should stand up for your rights. Though you may trust your spouse-to-be with all your heart, you should take the following steps to ensure that your prenuptial agreement protects you as well as your spouse.

- ◆ *Hire a well-qualified lawyer.* Your lawyer will be able to help you understand your property rights, advise you on the legal implications of your prenuptial agreement, and negotiate with your soon-to-be spouse's lawyer on your behalf. If you cannot afford a lawyer, ask your spouse-to-be to cover your prenup-related legal costs. This is standard practice when one spouse is significantly wealthier than the other.
- ◆ *Carefully consider the real-life consequences of your prenuptial agreement.* Make sure that you fully understand how your prenup will affect your property rights in real life. What will happen to you in the event of a divorce? What will happen to you if your spouse dies unexpectedly? Does the agreement take into account any career sacrifices you might make during your marriage? You should take the terms of your prenuptial agreement very seriously, since a prenup is a binding legal document with far-reaching legal ramifications.
- ◆ *Negotiate for the best terms you possibly can.* It is understandably a bit awkward to negotiate with the person you love and plan to marry. However, you cannot afford to sit back and simply sign whatever prenup terms are presented to you. You owe it to yourself to make sure that you will be adequately protected both during your marriage and in the event that your marriage ends through death or divorce.

◆ *Do not sign a prenup unless you are comfortable with each and every term.* If your spouse-to-be refuses to make even reasonable concessions to you in your prenuptial agreement, do not sign it. You will be *far* better off without a prenuptial agreement than with a prenuptial agreement that signs away all your rights.

Not convinced yet? Consider this true-life example.

EXAMPLE

Sun and her fiancé, Barry, were off to Las Vegas to tie the knot. On their way to the airport, Barry suggested that they stop off at his lawyer's office to sign a quick prenuptial agreement. Sun had not retained a lawyer and she had never seen even a draft of the prenuptial agreement before that time. Young and in love, Sun nevertheless signed a prenup providing that *all* of Barry's earnings would count as his separate property in the event of a divorce.

The Barry in question was Barry Bonds of the San Francisco Giants. His earnings went from $106,000 per year at the time of his marriage to Sun to *over eight million dollars* a year at the time of their divorce. Sun contested the prenuptial agreement and lost. The California Supreme Court ruled that the terms of the prenuptial agreement would be enforced even though Sun had no lawyer negotiating on her behalf at the time the agreement was signed. Sun's starry-eyed decision to sign the prenup Barry presented, no questions asked, cost her literally millions of dollars. Make sure you do not make the same mistake.

You could ruin your relationship by arguing over a prenup. Regardless of all the intellectual arguments in favor of a prenuptial agreement, some people remain firmly opposed to prenups on moral or philosophical grounds. Your spouse-to-be might view your sugges-tion of a prenup as a sign of mistrust or an indication of your lack of faith in the relationship. Depending on your soon-to-be spouse's view on prenuptial agreements, it is possible that simply raising the issue of a prenup could adversely affect your relationship.

Before you leap headfirst into negotiations over the terms of your prenup with your spouse-to-be, take a moment to anticipate how he or she is likely to react to the concept of a prenup. If you suspect that your loved one might take offense at the suggestion, be extremely sen-sitive with respect to when and where you bring up the prenup. (Raising the issue of a prenup when meeting your future in-laws for the first time, for example, might not go over too well.) An excellent resource on how to broach the topic of a prenup with your loved one is a book entitled *Prenups for Lovers: A Romantic Guide to Prenuptial Agreements,* by Arlene G. Dubin.

It may be that you and your spouse-to-be ultimately cannot come to any agreement on the issue of a prenup. If this happens in your case, you will be in the unenviable position of weighing your interest in a prenuptial agreement against your desire to formalize your rela-tionship through marriage. You will have to decide for yourself whether it is worth embarking on marriage when you and the person you love have such different views on an issue of relatively significant importance. Before ending the relationship for this reason alone, you might want to consider talking with a financial advisor to see whether you might be able to protect some of your financial rights *without* enter-ing into a prenuptial agreement.

EXAMPLE

Nora loved Andrew dearly, but she was afraid to marry him with-out a prenuptial agreement in place. Nora was most concerned about her mother, who had recently been diagnosed with Parkinson's disease. Nora's fears were that if she lost some or most of her assets in a divorce, she would not be able to provide for her mother in the years to come. Andrew, for his part, could not bear even to discuss the issue of a prenuptial agreement. Since he made more than Nora, Andrew could not even understand why she was fixated on having a prenuptial agreement.

At a loss as to what to do, Nora made an appointment with a financial advisor. Nora learned that she would be able to take care of her mother without having a prenuptial agreement in place, simply by establishing a trust for the benefit of her mother. The trust solved Nora's problem and she no longer felt a prenuptial agreement would be necessary.

You could run up enormous legal bills if you opt for a prenuptial agreement. Since most lawyers do not work for free, entering into a prenuptial agreement is probably going to cost you a few hundred to a few thousand dollars (depending on your financial circumstances and the issues covered by your prenup). The idea of forking out big bucks for legal fees is probably quite unappealing, particularly since it would be much more fun to spend the money on a longer honeymoon or a stretch limousine for your wedding day.

As painful as it is to pay the legal fees associated with a prenuptial agreement, the reality is that a prenup will more than pay for itself if life ever takes a turn for the worse. Some financial experts estimate that every dollar spent on a prenup can save you *thousands* of dollars in legal fees if your marriage ends in divorce. Moreover, you can limit the costs associated with a prenup by reaching a basic agreement on the terms with your spouse-to-be before ever setting foot in a lawyer's office. You can even shop around for a lawyer who will handle your prenuptial agreement for a flat fee instead of charging by the hour for the negotiation and drafting work.

To put it simply, there are many good reasons why you might decide against a prenuptial agreement. Saving money on lawyers' fees, however, should not be one of them.

When You Should Seriously Consider a Prenup

While prenuptial agreements are no longer just for millionaires and movie stars, the truth of the matter is that some people need prenuptial agreements more than others. You should *seriously* consider a prenuptial agreement if any of the following situations apply to you.

You will be bringing a substantial amount of wealth into the marriage. If you are fortunate enough to fall into this category, you probably already know why a prenuptial agreement is a good idea for you. It can protect your assets in the event of a divorce, by specifying exactly how your assets will be divided between you and your spouse. A prenuptial agreement can also address the issue of spousal support so that you will not be bound to subsidize your spouse's lifestyle even after your marriage has ended.

EXAMPLE

Roy had saved up nearly half a million dollars while waiting for the right girl to come along. A math whiz with a knack for timing the market, Roy knew that he would have to act fast when he met Leah, an off-broadway actress whose next production was scheduled to be in California. Roy proposed over a pre-theater dinner just two weeks after they met and Leah moved into Roy's apartment that very evening. Realizing that he was getting a bit swept off his feet, Roy decided he should meet with a lawyer to take care of the practical and legal end of his upcoming marriage. Roy explained to his lawyer that if his marriage ended, he wanted to be able to keep his half-a-million dollar nest egg free and clear. He also wanted to provide enough so that Leah would be able to manage financially for at least a few years after their marriage had ended.

Roy's lawyer proposed an agreement whereby all of Roy's premarital earnings would remain his separate property in the event of a divorce. Roy's lawyer also suggested that Roy and Leah come up with a spousal support figure that would make sense in the event that the couple divorced. Leah asked Roy to provide her with $3,500 of tax-free spousal support each month for two years. This money would allow Leah to pay the rent and cover her basic living expenses until she was back on her feet. Roy did the math and realized that this would amount to $84,000—or about $160,000 before taxes. After a little back and forth, Leah agreed to $3,000 of tax-free spousal support each month for two years in exchange for waiving her interest in Roy's premarital earnings and any other money he earned during their marriage. Roy was happy with this arrangement, as was Leah.

You have children from a previous marriage. When you have children from a previous marriage, you have more to worry about than whether your children will adjust well to your new relationship. You also have to think about whether you can continue to provide for your children at a level they are accustomed to and ensure that your children will receive an appropriate share of your estate in the event of your death. A prenuptial agreement is very helpful in this regard because it can provide that your spouse waives his or her elective share of your estate, so your assets can be distributed to your children in accordance with the provisions of your will. A prenuptial agreement can also establish your right to contribute as much as money as you wish to support your children during your marriage.

Abby had three children from a previous marriage when she met Ethan. Abby earned a good living as a chiropractor, bending people's backs back into shape all day long. Ethan earned even more as an editor-in-chief of the city's largest newspaper. The couple looked forward to wedded bliss and the cushy lifestyle they would enjoy as a result of combining their households and their incomes. Abby gave no thought whatsoever to a prenuptial agreement until Ethan one day asked her about a bill for the children's tennis lessons that he found lying on the dining table. She realized that Ethan had no idea how much of her income went to support her children. Between clothes, toys, and after-school activities, there was not that much left for Abby to save each month. Abby was concerned that Ethan would pressure her to limit her spending on the children. Ethan became a bit nervous that much of his income would end up being spent on the children's seemingly endless needs.

The couple decided that a prenuptial agreement was in order. The two soon came to an agreement providing that Abby and Ethan would each maintain separate accounts that they could use any way they pleased. Ethan would pay two-thirds of the household expenses, while Abby would pay one-third. The agreement allowed Abby the freedom to continue spending on her children to her heart's content, even after her marriage to Ethan.

You or your spouse-to-be owns a business or professional practice, or plans on starting one during your marriage. Businesses and professional practices can lead to costly and contentious disputes if divorce ever rears its ugly head. (For more information on this, please see pages 41 through 44 of Chapter Two.) A prenuptial agreement empowers you to avoid these potential problems entirely by specifying exactly how your business or professional practice will be valued and divided in the event of a divorce. A prenuptial agreement can also address how business earnings and debt will be handled during the marriage.

EXAMPLE

Logan wanted to open a small bed and breakfast inn in his Vermont hometown. Hanna, his soon-to-be wife, thought this was a great idea. However, Hanna was terrified that the bed and breakfast inn would consume all of their savings and bury the couple in debt until it became a truly profitable enterprise.

She suggested that the two of them enter into a prenuptial agreement to address these issues. Logan agreed that he would sink no more than $30,000 of their marital funds into the bed and breakfast inn. He also agreed that he would not take out any loans for which he would be personally liable. Hanna, for her part, agreed to exert her best efforts to ensure that the bed and breakfast inn would be a success, including offering up her services as a cook and housekeeper.

While Logan and Hanna were quite confident that their marriage would always be rewarding even if the business was not, they thought it would be best to agree on what would happen to the bed and breakfast inn in the event of a divorce. The prenuptial agreement provided that the inn would be sold immediately, with the proceeds divided equally between Hanna and Logan.

You expect to receive sizeable gifts or inheritances during your marriage. Even if you have no doubts whatsoever about your upcoming marriage, your relatives might have their reservations. You probably do not want their hesitation about your marriage to get in the way of their generosity to you. Having a prenuptial agreement in place can provide your loved ones with reassurance that their gifts will remain with you even in the event of a divorce.

EXAMPLE

Matthew was a hopeless romantic who had just presented his beloved Emma with a two-carat engagement ring, tucked inside a matchbox from the restaurant where they had enjoyed their first dinner together. Matthew's persnickety Aunt Olivia had not-so-nice things to say about almost everyone, but even she could find no flaws in Emma.

Much as Aunt Olivia took to Emma, however, she was concerned about leaving the bulk of her estate to Matthew. She had seen one too many marriages turn ugly in her day. She wanted to ensure that her estate would remain intact and in Matthew's hands regardless of what transpired in his personal life. Emma (the child of divorced parents herself) understood Aunt Olivia's concerns and (in a testament to Emma's unimpeachable character) did not take any offense. Emma herself suggested a prenuptial agreement, providing that anything Matthew inherited during their marriage would count as his separate property in the event of a divorce, even if he used that inheritance to support the couple during their marriage. Aunt Olivia could not have been more delighted. She immediately rewrote her will to leave her entire estate to Matthew.

You are a little older than the average soon-to-be newlywed. If you are an older adult on the verge of tying the knot, you probably have much more to consider than your younger counterparts. You might have built up a sizeable asset base over the years and you may have grown children (or even grandchildren) whose needs you must take into account. You must also seriously think about issues like planning for your retirement and long-term care. For all of these reasons, a prenuptial agreement is a very wise idea.

After her husband, Hank, passed away, Elizabeth desperately missed the friendship and companionship of a life partner. So Elizabeth began dating again, much to the surprise of her three children and the amusement of her eight-year-old granddaughter, Bethany. Bethany was the first to know when Elizabeth found Jim, a special new someone Elizabeth wanted to hang onto for all the years to come. While Bethany adored Jim, Elizabeth's children were not too happy with the idea of a new stepfather. Her children were also worried about the legal consequences of Elizabeth's planned marriage to Jim. How would this affect their inheritance rights? Would Elizabeth be on the hook if Jim ended up needing years of expensive nursing home care?

Elizabeth loved her children dearly. She wanted to allay their concerns, so that they could welcome Jim into the family with open arms and no hesitations. So Elizabeth proposed that she and Jim enter into a prenuptial agreement. Their prenuptial agreement provided that she and Jim would each waive any automatic rights they had in the other's estate. The agreement further provided that Elizabeth and Jim would each be independently responsible for their own long-term care or other health-related expenses.

You or your spouse-to-be has a great deal of debt or high liability exposure. When one or both of you is saddled with substantial amounts of debt, it is very important to decide in advance who will be responsible for paying down that debt once you have tied the knot. You might decide that you will share responsibility for those debts, and will use marital property (money you earn during your marriage) to cover the debts. Or you might decide that you will each be solely responsible for your own debts, and that no marital property will be used to pay those debts. Coming to agreement on these issues before your marriage will protect your relationship from debt-related resentment or confusion down the line. A prenuptial agreement can specify who will be liable for debts and other liabilities incurred before and during your marriage. In addition, a prenuptial agreement can address asset protection strategies—such as keeping certain assets in one spouse's name only to ensure that those assets cannot be reached by the other spouse's creditors.

EXAMPLE

Natalie was an obstetrician in her own private practice. While Natalie loved the business of bringing new babies into the world, she was not too happy about the high liability associated with her profession. (Obstetricians are frequently sued for malpractice— much more so than most physicians.) She bought the best malpractice insurance she could afford, but she still worried that one adverse judgment could leave her bankrupt.

Todd, Natalie's fiancé, was just as concerned as Natalie. He proposed that he and Natalie enter into a prenuptial agreement, providing that most of their assets would be kept in Todd's name only. This would ensure that the assets would be safe in the event that Natalie was successfully sued for a sum in excess of her insurance coverage. The agreement further provided that in the event of a divorce, all of the assets they acquired during their marriage—including the assets in Todd's name only—would be divided evenly between Todd and Natalie. Natalie was delighted with the arrangement and with her newfound financial security.

You plan on making career sacrifices to raise a family or to advance the career of your spouse-to-be. More and more people these days are finding that it is very difficult to have it all—two successful careers, beautiful children, a happy home, and a well-stocked bank account. For many people, the only practical solution is for one spouse to take a step back professionally—whether by dropping out of the workforce entirely or choosing a job with better hours—in order to raise happy children or to advance the other spouse's career. The usual understanding is that the sacrificing spouse will be well taken care of financially by the other spouse, but this understanding is often forgotten when the marriage fails and divorce proceedings are underway. A prenuptial agreement can guarantee that the sacrificing spouse will be appropriately compensated if the marriage ends in divorce.

EXAMPLE

Monica had a promising career as an associate at one of the country's top law firms when she met Nicholas, a consultant who spent his vacations trekking through Nepal and climbing large mountains. Monica fell in love so quickly that she could hardly focus on the securities fraud cases she had once found so interesting. All she could think about was Nicholas and their life together. Nicholas soon proposed and Monica's days became a whirlwind of gown fittings, meetings with caterers, and completing gift registries. When Nicholas asked Monica if she would be willing to move to Texas, where he had received an incredible offer to head up a new consulting company, Monica did not even think twice before saying yes. She knew this would mean leaving her job, but Nicholas's compensation package would more than make up for the loss of her salary.

While Monica had become quite swept up in her new romance and upcoming wedding, she had not completely forgotten everything she learned in law school. She asked Nicholas to enter into a prenuptial agreement, providing her half of everything he earned during their marriage, plus a decent amount in spousal support for a few years. Monica knew that she would have a difficult time reestablishing herself in her legal career if she walked out on her job to marry Nicholas. She wanted to be sure that she would be protected financially in the event that her marriage did not go as smoothly as she had hoped. Nicholas gladly signed the agreement, because he understood that he was asking Monica to make a serious career sacrifice for his sake. He wanted nothing more than for his bride to feel secure in her decision.

You or your spouse-to-be will be earning a professional degree or license during your marriage. The law with respect to how professional licenses and degrees are treated in the event of a divorce is still very much in evolution. (For more on this, see the discussion on professional licenses and degrees on page 41-44.) A prenuptial agreement can provide some much-needed certainty on the issue. If you plan to support your spouse while he or she earns a professional license or degree, you might want a prenuptial agreement to specify how you will be compensated in the event of a divorce. If you are the one who will be earning the license or degree, you might want to agree in advance that the license or degree will not be considered marital property in the event of a divorce.

EXAMPLE

Steven had just received his acceptance letter from Harvard Business School when he met Serena, a long-legged yoga student whose spiritual philosophy moved him. Steven was eager to tie the knot so that Serena could accompany him to Cambridge in the fall. However, he was nervous that his business school degree would be considered marital property if he and Serena were married while he was in school.

He asked Serena to sign a prenuptial agreement, providing that the value of the degree would not be taken into account in the event of a divorce. Serena usually paid little attention to financial and legal matters, preferring instead to focus on her spiritual well-being, but she thought she had better think things through before signing a prenuptial agreement. After a few discussions with her detail-oriented mother, Serena proposed that Steven agree that she would receive 15% of his earnings for three years if they divorced soon after Steven completed business school. Serena knew that they would not accumulate much in the way of marital property while Steven was in school. If Steven left her when he graduated from business school, Serena would end up with almost nothing in the way of marital property. Steven was impressed with Serena's financial foresight and readily agreed to her proposed terms.

5

Doing it Right:
Seven Rules
for a Rock-Solid Prenup

If you and your spouse-to-be decide that a prenuptial agreement makes sense in your case, it is not enough simply to scribble your understanding down on a scrap piece of paper. Rather, you must follow certain established rules when negotiating and memorializing your agreement. This chapter explains the seven most important rules for a rock-solid prenuptial agreement. If you ignore these rules, you could end up with a prenuptial agreement that would never stand up in court.

Rule #1: Put your prenuptial agreement in writing and make sure you and your spouse-to-be both sign it. You might think it is unnecessary to have a formal prenuptial agreement in place, specifying each spouse's rights in the event of debt, divorce, and death. Why can't you and your loved one simply sit down and reach an understanding on your own without going through all the bother and expense of having lawyers put it in writing? The answer is simple. Most courts will not enforce a prenuptial agreement unless it is *in writing* and *signed* by both spouses.

Russ and his fiancé, Charlotte, were both musicians who shared a love of jazz and a strong distaste for lawyers. Before they married, they had a long heart-to-heart about the not-so-romantic practical side of marriage—death, divorce, debt, and money in general. Charlotte and Russ agreed that if they ever divorced, they would divide everything they earned while they were married equally between them. Russ and Charlotte also promised to rewrite their wills to leave their entire estates to one another. Neither Russ nor Charlotte discussed their agreement with a lawyer and they did not bother to write anything down. Both of them felt that their word was enough.

Charlotte rewrote her will, just as she had promised. But Russ never got around to rewriting his before he was tragically killed in a motorcycle accident. Charlotte learned from the lawyer for Russ's estate that his will made no mention of her whatsoever. Because the *prenuptial agreement* that she and Russ had agreed to was not in writing, there was no way for Charlotte to enforce Russ's promise to rewrite his will to leave her all his assets. Charlotte was therefore entitled to nothing more than her elective share of Russ's estate—which, in their state, was only one third of his estate. The remainder of Russ's estate went to Russ's parents, who were the only people named in his will.

Rule #2: Hire a lawyer to advise you on your prenuptial agreement and make sure that your spouse-to-be does the same. You might be tempted to save on legal fees and enter into a do-it-yourself prenuptial agreement with your loved one. Though you might consider this biased advice (since it is coming from someone who makes her living practicing matrimonial law), not hiring a lawyer for the purposes of your prenuptial agreement is penny-wise and pound foolish.

Lawyers serve several important purposes in the context of prenuptial agreements. Your lawyer will:

◆ explain your legal rights to you and help you understand how your prenuptial agreement will affect those rights;

◆ keep you from signing an agreement that is overly lopsided in favor of your spouse-to-be;

◆ provide you with bargaining power by negotiating better terms on your behalf;

◆ help you comply with the financial disclosure requirements (see Rule #3);

◆ make sure that you receive appropriate financial disclosure from your spouse-to-be; and,

◆ take all necessary steps to ensure that your prenuptial agreement will stand up in court.

Not only should you go out and retain a lawyer, but you should make sure that your spouse-to-be does the same. If your spouse-to-be cannot afford a lawyer, you should cover the legal bills yourself. (Trust me, this is a very wise investment.) The last thing you want is for your spouse to challenge the agreement down the line on the grounds that he or she did not understand the legal consequences of your prenup. You should make certain that your spouse-to-be hires a lawyer who is just as competent as your own, and that his or her lawyer is completely independent of you. For example, this would not be a good time to call in that favor from your cousin Bill, a criminal lawyer who happens to do a little family law on the side. Otherwise, your spouse-to-be could later claim that he or she did not have the benefit of independent legal counsel, since the lawyer you provided was biased in your favor.

When each spouse-to-be has his or her own independent lawyer, it is much more likely that their agreement will stand up in court. Having separate and well-qualified lawyers ensures that each spouse-to-be will understand what he or she is signing (because it is a lawyer's obligation to explain the consequences of each and every term of a prenuptial agreement) and will also have the opportunity to negotiate for more favorable terms before signing the agreement.

EXAMPLE

Alexis was a very well-endowed young woman (her trust fund was larger than the gross national products of some developing nations). When Alexis announced her engagement to Joshua, a man who considered his friends and family to be his greatest riches, Alexis's family immediately demanded that the commoner sign a prenuptial agreement. Joshua said that he would gladly sign anything in order to put their minds at ease, but Alexis insisted that he hire a lawyer to look over the agreement and negotiate on his behalf. So Joshua begrudgingly retained a lawyer and Alexis paid the bill.

Joshua's lawyer looked over the agreement proposed by Alexis's family and carefully explained the terms to Joshua. Joshua was surprised to learn that the agreement essentially provided that Joshua would get nothing in the event of a divorce—not even spousal support—even if they were married for twenty years. While Joshua was not troubled by this (since he felt in his heart that he and Alexis would never part ways), he was very hurt by the provision that left him with nothing in the event that Alexis died.

Joshua discussed this with Alexis (who had left the details of the agreement to her lawyer) and the two agreed that the provision was incredibly unfair. Alexis instructed her lawyer to redraft the agreement to provide that Joshua would receive half of her entire estate in the event of her death, with the other half going to charity. Alexis's family was not pleased, but Alexis and Joshua were comfortable with the arrangement. Joshua was grateful that he had a lawyer to *translate* the agreement into plain

English for him. Had it not been for the lawyer, Joshua would have signed away all of his rights without even realizing it.

Rule #3: Provide your spouse-to-be with the complete details of your personal finances and ask for the same in return. Comprehensive financial disclosure is perhaps the most important prerequisite to a valid prenuptial agreement. This is because you and your spouse-to-be need to have a thorough understanding of one another's financial situation before you can negotiate the terms of your prenuptial agreement in fairness. For example, you probably would not agree to waive all spousal support claims if you knew that your soon-to-be spouse was a millionaire and not the starving artist he claimed to be. Or you would not agree to be jointly responsible for all debts incurred during the marriage if it turned out that your spouse had a secret gambling problem and had already accumulated tens of thousands of dollars in casino debts. The fact of the matter is that unless you and your spouse-to-be provide one another with thorough details of your personal finances, your prenup will not be enforceable.

You and your spouse-to-be should each disclose:

◆ your income;
◆ your assets and liabilities; and,
◆ any other pertinent financial information, such as an expected inheritance or a financially significant impending business deal.

Should you be concerned that your spouse-to-be might share some of this information with friends or family, you could ask your lawyer to have a confidentiality agreement in place before handing over your financial disclosure statement. A confidentiality agreement can provide that your spouse-to-be may only share your financial disclosure statement with certain people, such as his or her lawyer and accountant.

If you fail to provide your spouse-to-be with *complete* financial disclosure, a court could later invalidate your prenuptial agreement.

Jordan was a newspaper reporter whose specialty was unraveling white collar crime stories. His own personal finances were in impeccable order and he was only too happy to provide his fiancé, Alicia, with a download of his Quicken files when it came time for the two of them to enter into a prenuptial agreement. Jordan's Quicken files provided Alicia with incredibly detailed information about his personal finances—down to how much money he spent on hot dogs and magazines each month. The only thing missing from Jordan's files was any mention of his small savings account in the Cayman Islands, containing close to a million dollars. Jordan had amassed these riches through bribes from businessmen who were willing to pay almost anything to keep their names off of the front page.

Alicia knew nothing of this Cayman Islands account or Jordan's illegal bribery scheme. From what she could tell from his Quicken files, Jordan was nothing more than a humble newspaper reporter who managed to save just a few hundred dollars per month in his 401(k) account. Because Alicia felt sorry for Jordan since he worked so hard and appeared to make so little, the couple entered into a prenuptial agreement providing that Alicia would actually pay Jordan spousal support in the event of a divorce. Jordan filed for divorce a few years later, fully expecting to collect a few extra dollars each month from Alicia. To Jordan's shock, Alicia moved to nullify their prenuptial agreement. (Jordan had left a statement from his Cayman Islands account in his pocket on a day when Alicia was taking in the dry cleaning.) The court held their prenuptial agreement null and void since Jordan had failed to provide Alicia with full financial disclosure. (The court also alerted the district attorney to Jordan's illicit money-making activities.)

Rule #4: Do not force your spouse-to-be to enter into a prenuptial agreement. Your prenuptial agreement will only stand up in court if you and your spouse-to-be both enter into the agreement voluntarily and with a full understanding of the consequences of the agreement. If you coerce your soon-to-be spouse into signing a prenup, you will likely end up with an unenforceable prenuptial agreement *and* a very unhappy spouse-to-be. Putting unacceptable pressure to enter into a prenup by emotionally or physically abusing your spouse-to-be until he or she breaks down and signs the agreement allows the court to throw out the agreement. Refusing to marry your loved one without a prenuptial agreement in place, however, is perfectly acceptable behavior.

EXAMPLE

Rachel came from a very conservative Catholic family that was very well respected in her community. She considered herself to be quite a good girl and had never given her family reason to be anything but proud of her. All of that changed after her fiancé, Parker, popped the question. Rachel broke a rather important rule one Saturday afternoon and she soon learned she was pregnant with Parker's child. Rachel pleaded with Parker to move up the wedding date. Parker agreed on one condition—that Rachel would sign whatever prenuptial agreement Parker presented. Rachel signed the prenup without even reading it and the two were married in time for Rachel to claim that her baby was born just a few weeks early.

Rachel never looked back at the prenuptial agreement until years later, when Parker filed for divorce. She realized that she had signed away basically all her rights to everything Parker earned during their marriage. If the agreement were enforced, Rachel would hardly be able to support herself. So Rachel hired the best lawyer in town and challenged the prenuptial agreement, claiming that Parker forced her to sign it. Rachel won, and walked away with half of everything Parker earned during their marriage, plus spousal support.

A prenuptial agreement must be a two-way street. Either you must both enter into it voluntarily or you must take your chances without one.

Rule #5: Take care of your prenuptial agreement well in advance of your wedding. Do not wait until after you have paid the deposit for the caterer and sent out all your wedding invitations to pop the next big question. When all the wedding arrangements have been made, there is a great deal of pressure for even the most self-assured bride or groom to sign whatever legal document the other proposes just to make it to the big day. You do not want to put your spouse-to-be in the awkward position of considering a prenuptial agreement when friends and family have already purchased plane tickets and wedding gifts.

The better approach by far is to bring up the issue of a prenuptial agreement well in advance of your wedding. This way, you and your spouse-to-be can both focus on the nitty-gritty terms of the prenup without worrying whether the negotiations will delay the wedding. If you do not give your spouse-to-be enough lead time before the wedding to consider the significant legal and financial issues raised by a prenuptial agreement, your spouse-to-be could later challenge the validity of your prenup by arguing that he or she felt pressured to sign the agreement.

EXAMPLE

Amelia had envisioned her wedding day ever since she was a little girl. When Caleb proposed, she pulled out her archives of *Bride* magazine and began the much-awaited task of planning her big day. Amelia agonized over whether the floral arrangements should include lilies or roses; attempted to color-coordinate her invitations with her wedding favors; and tried on no fewer than two hundred wedding gowns before settling on the perfect one. Amelia had already sent out hand-calligraphied invitations and completed their wedding registry when Caleb first raised the issue of a prenuptial agreement.

Caleb suggested that Amelia should receive a lump sum payment of $20,000 in lieu of her share of marital property and spousal support if they ever divorced. This sounded fair enough to Amelia (whose daddy had always paid all the bills for her). She was too wrapped up in wedding planning to focus on what she viewed as legal mumbo-jumbo. Moreover, since she had already told all her friends and family about her upcoming nuptials, she had no intention of doing anything that would rock the boat and jeopardize her chances of a dream wedding.

Fast forward ten years. Caleb had become a very successful real estate developer and Amelia had become a consummate homemaker and devoted mother. She had long since forgotten about the prenuptial agreement she hastily signed as a young bride-to-be when one day—out of the blue—Caleb served her with divorce papers and a check in the amount of $20,000. Amelia was horrified. She had grown accustomed to living in the lap of luxury and she had taken care of the house and the children while Caleb was working his way to the top. There was no way that $20,000 would enable her to support herself for even a few months.

Amelia retained a lawyer to challenge the prenuptial agreement. She presented evidence that she signed the prenup just a few weeks before the wedding and was too concerned about the potential embarrassment of a canceled wedding to be able to negotiate the terms of her prenup in earnest. In essence, Amelia claimed she felt she had no choice but to sign the agreement. The court agreed with Amelia, and she ended up walking away with half of the millions that Caleb had earned during their marriage.

Rule #6: Make sure that your prenuptial agreement is fair to your spouse-to-be. Both to ensure the enforceability of your prenuptial agreement and for the sake of your upcoming marriage, make sure that your prenup is fair to your spouse-to-be. Do not ask your loved one to sign away basically all his or her property rights in order to have the privilege of being your spouse. Just remember, you love your soon-to-be spouse and you owe it to him or her to strike a fair deal. If your prenup is totally lopsided in your favor, a court may very well overturn your prenup in the event it is ever challenged. Courts do not like to enforce agreements that are fundamentally unfair to one side.

EXAMPLE

Spencer and his business partner, Marisol, had built up a tremendously successful interior design company together. Spencer and Marisol had each invested $30,000 of their own money into the business and they had worked side-by-side on their most important projects. One night, while debating over carpet samples, sparks began to fly and Spencer and Marisol went from business partners to life partners.

Spencer proposed within weeks. He explained to Marisol that he would not be able to continue working with her so closely in the event their romance fizzled, and so he asked her to sign a prenuptial agreement providing that the business would be his to keep in the event of a divorce. All Marisol would get would be a reimbursement of her $30,000. Marisol was normally a tough negotiator, never paying even a penny more than necessary for custom upholstery or wall-to-wall carpeting. But the stars in her eyes kept her from thinking straight on the issue of her prenup, so she went ahead and signed the agreement.

Spencer turned out to be the most loyal and devoted of husbands. Marisol, however, soon began to feel bored with the monotony of monogamy. She began to experiment with men half her age and soon ended up filing for divorce. Spencer handed her a check for $30,000 and presented her with papers handing over the entire business to him, per the prenup. Marisol balked and hired a lawyer, who challenged the prenuptial agreement as unconscionable. The judge agreed with Marisol—it was tremendously unfair for Marisol to have to give up the fruits of all her hard work to Spencer just because their marriage had not been as successful as their business.

Rule #7: Update your prenuptial agreement regularly during your marriage. Do not consider your prenuptial agreement as written in stone for all the years of your married life. Instead, you should revisit your prenuptial agreement regularly to make sure that its terms still make sense in light of the circumstances of your life. A prenuptial agreement that works well when you are in your early years of marriage and still getting to know one another's hidden quirks might not fit well after you have had two children and your spouse has given up his or her career to be a full-time parent. If fairness alone does not move you to update your prenuptial agreement from time to time, concerns about the continued enforceability of your prenup most definitely should. Courts are increasingly considering whether the terms of prenuptial agreements are fair as of the time of the divorce when deciding whether or not to enforce them. When circumstances have changed a great deal between the time the prenup was signed and the time of a divorce, courts recognize that the terms of a prenup may no longer be just or appropriate.

EXAMPLE

Kirsten and her husband, Noel, had signed a prenup providing that they would each keep their earnings in separate bank accounts during their marriage and that their respective earnings would count as separate property in the event of a divorce.

Five years into their marriage, Kirsten and Noel had grown to love and trust one another so much that they no longer maintained separate accounts. They had even taken out a mortgage together, on which they were jointly liable. When Kirsten learned she was pregnant, she decided it was time to talk to Noel about renegotiating the terms of the prenup. Kirsten was concerned that she would be left with hardly anything in the event of a divorce, particularly since her own earnings would likely decline when she prioritized mothering over her career.

Noel agreed that it was time for a change. He wanted to make sure that Kirsten would feel secure enough about their financial arrangement to spend as much time as possible with their new baby, even if that meant quitting her job or taking a part-time position at a less prestigious company. Noel proposed that he and Kirsten divide equally everything that the two of them earned during their marriage and that the couple would continue to maintain joint bank accounts for the duration of their marriage. Because Kirsten's share of Noel's marital earnings would amount to a significant sum, Kirsten agreed that she would not seek spousal support in the event of a divorce. Kirsten and Noel were both happy that their agreement reflected the new reality of their marriage.

6

Anatomy of a Prenup: Topics to Consider

As long as you are careful to follow the seven rules for a rock-solid prenup outlined in Chapter Five, the specific contents of your prenup are entirely up to you and your future spouse. The beauty of a prenuptial agreement is that you and your spouse-to-be are free to decide what you will include in your prenup and what you will leave out. This chapter helps you start to think about what issues you would like addressed in your prenuptial agreement and the terms of your prenup. You should use the information in this chapter as a springboard for discussions with your lawyer and spouse-to-be regarding what you would ideally like to see included (and what you would prefer to have left out) in your prenuptial agreement. (To see how it all comes together, take a look at the sample prenuptial agreement provided in Chapter Seven.)

Divorce Provisions

Because so many people view prenuptial agreements primarily as a form of *divorce insurance*, divorce-related prenuptial provisions are usually considered first and foremost. However, bear in mind that prenuptial agreements serve many purposes in addition to establishing each spouse's property rights in the event of a divorce.

THE DIVISION OF MARITAL PROPERTY

Any prenuptial agreement worth the paper it is written on should specify what counts as marital property and how it will be divided between you and your spouse in the event of a divorce. You and your spouse-to-be are free to designate any of your current or future property as marital or separate. The important thing is to make sure that the agreement is very clear in specifying what counts as marital property and what counts as separate property. You could agree that none of your property will constitute marital property in the event of a divorce. You could also agree that *all* of your property counts as marital property.

Regardless of how you decide to define marital property, be sure that your prenuptial agreement addresses all of the following categories of property (unless any particular category of property is inapplicable given your situation):

◆ premarital property (property you or your spouse earned or acquired before your marriage);

◆ property earned by you or your spouse during your marriage;

◆ pensions, 401(k) plans, and other retirement benefits;

◆ stock options;

◆ gifts from one spouse to the other;

◆ gifts received from third parties (including wedding gifts);

◆ engagement and wedding rings;

◆ professional licenses and degrees;

◆ professional practices, including professional goodwill;

◆ businesses;

◆ shares of closely held corporations;

◆ intellectual property (for example, a book written by your spouse or a new medical device you invent);

◆ income received during the marriage from separate property (for example, rental income from a house you inherited from your grandmother);

◆ the passive appreciation of separate property that occurs during the marriage (for example, the growth of stocks you owned before you were married); and,

◆ the active appreciation of separate property that occurs during the marriage (for example, the increase in value of a condominium that results from the weekends you spend renovating the condominium during your marriage).

You should also consider specifying in your prenuptial agreement how complex types of marital property—such as businesses or professional practices—will be *valued* in the event of a divorce. For example, your agreement could provide that you and your spouse-to-be will jointly appoint one valuation expert to value your spouse's accounting practice and any attendant goodwill, and the valuation will be binding upon both of you in the event of a divorce.

You should also consider addressing the mechanics of how the business will be divided in the event of a divorce. For example, you and your spouse-to-be could agree that the bistro the two of you just opened will be sold in the event of a divorce, with the proceeds to be divided equally between you.

Your prenuptial agreement should then set forth how marital property will be divided between you and your spouse in the event of a divorce. For example, your prenup could provide that all marital property will be divided equally between you and your spouse in the event of a divorce. Your prenuptial agreement could instead provide that you will receive 75% of all marital property, while your spouse-to-be will receive only 25%. Prenuptial agreements are nice because you and your spouse-to-be can agree on a division of marital property that makes sense in your particular case.

To be on the safe side, your prenup should also address the question of what happens if separate property is mixed with marital property. One approach is for your prenup to provide that if either of you contributes separate property for marital purposes (for example, by using your inheritance funds to put a down payment on a house you will both live in during your marriage), the person who contributes the separate property will be reimbursed in the event of a divorce. This will protect both you and your spouse-to-be from messy separate property claims in a divorce. To give you some context for all of this, consider two different examples to see how the division of marital property can be handled in a prenup.

EXAMPLE 1

Ryan and Allison viewed marriage as a merger of their emotional lives, but not their financial lives. Ryan had a booming construction firm and Allison was a fourth-grade teacher whose lunchtime day trading had enabled her to build up quite an impressive nest egg. Both Ryan and Allison were very uncomfortable with the idea that either of them could lose much of what he or she had worked so hard to build if their marriage hit the rocks. So Ryan and Allison agreed that they would each contribute 25% of their pre-tax earnings to a joint account for their mutual benefit. This account would be used to pay their living expenses and for their shared savings. Any funds in the joint account would be divided evenly between Ryan and Allison in the event of a divorce. The remainder of their assets, including Ryan's construction firm and Allison's brokerage account, would remain off-limits for property division purposes in the event of a divorce.

EXAMPLE 2

Sean and Audrey had a very different take on marriage. The two viewed marriage as a serious financial commitment, not just a romantic one. They planned to merge all their assets—including premarital assets, gifts, and inheritances—and to share and share alike during their marriage. Their prenuptial agreement provided that marital property would consist of everything owned by either spouse at the end of their marriage—a reasonable arrangement since neither Sean nor Audrey had any real assets going into the marriage. Because Sean expected that he would have a much great earning capacity than Audrey (since he held an M.B.A. from Stanford), he agreed that Audrey would receive 60% of all marital property.

You and your spouse-to-be might decide that designating certain categories of property as marital property and specifying how that property will be divided is a bit too unwieldy or unpredictable for your tastes. One alternative is to agree that the wealthier spouse will provide a lump-sum payment to the other spouse in lieu of a distribution of marital property.

EXAMPLE

Brett earned half a million dollars per year as a tax advisor to blue chip companies. He had amassed over two million dollars in investment holdings and he expected his income and his assets would continue to grow in the years to come. He wanted to be fair to his fiancé, Claudia, but he also wanted to be able to know in advance what he would owe to her in the event of a divorce. So he offered her distributive payments instead of her share of marital property. If they were married for less than five years, Claudia would receive $250,000; if they were married for anywhere between five and ten years, Claudia would receive $500,000; and, if they were married for more than ten years, Claudia would receive $750,000. Claudia considered Brett's offer to be quite generous, and it made her feel much more comfortable giving up her career to settle down with Brett.

Spousal Support

Be certain that your prenuptial agreement addresses the issue of spousal support in some way. Your prenuptial agreement should ideally specify the following.

◆ *When one spouse will owe the other spouse support.* Your agreement should set forth the circumstances under which one spouse will owe the other support payments. For example, your agreement could provide that no spousal support will be owed unless your marriage lasts for at least four years.

◆ *How much support will be due.* You can put down dollar figures or specify a formula for calculating how much spousal support one of you will owe the other.

◆ *How long spousal support will last.* Your agreement should indicate the duration of spousal support. For example, you may want to provide one year of spousal support for every two years of marriage.

◆ *When spousal support will end.* Your agreement could provide that spousal support payments will terminate once the less well-off spouse's income reaches a certain level or as soon as the less well-off spouse begins living with someone in a romantic relationship. Your agreement could also deviate from the default rules that spousal support terminates once the less well-off spouse remarries or the wealthier spouse dies.

◆ *Whether spousal support will include the cost of health insurance.* Your agreement could provide that one spouse will provide the other with health insurance for a specified period of time. Particularly if one of you will be relying on the other's employer-subsidized health insurance during your marriage, it is important to address the issue of health insurance so that the dependent spouse is not left without insurance coverage in the event the marriage ends.

◆ *The tax status of spousal support payments.* The usual rule (subject to certain exceptions) is that spousal support payments are taxable to the payee and tax-deductible for the payer. You could provide in your agreement that spousal support will not count as taxable income for the payee.

The most important concern for many people is the amount of spousal support that will be owed. One possible option is for you and your spouse-to-be each to waive your rights to support in the event of a divorce—in other words, to provide for zero spousal support in your prenup regardless of the circumstances. Be aware that courts in some states will not enforce a blanket waiver of spousal support. As a practical matter, this means that a court might disregard the terms of your prenuptial agreement and order spousal support if it is warranted given the particular facts of your case at the time of your divorce. You should also be aware that no state will enforce a waiver of spousal support if it will have the effect of leaving one spouse completely destitute and dependent on public assistance to support him- or herself. This is because spouses have a legal duty to support one another. This obligation extends even after the marriage has ended. If your prenuptial agreement provides that you and your spouse will each waive your rights to spousal support in the event of a divorce, make sure that your agreement specifies that each spouse will be perfectly capable of supporting him- or herself in the event of a divorce.

EXAMPLE

Lindsay and Darren were both law students who looked forward to six-figure incomes after they passed their bar exams. Soon after Darren proposed (in the law school cafeteria), Lindsay brought up the issue of a prenuptial agreement. Among the many issues Lindsay thought they should cover in their prenup was spousal support. She proposed that they each waive their rights to support in the event of a divorce, a provision to which Darren readily agreed. To help ensure that the provision would be enforceable in the event of a divorce, Lindsay's lawyer included a discussion in the prenup of the training and education that Darren and Lindsay had each received. Lindsay's lawyer wanted the prenuptial agreement to demonstrate on its face that Lindsay and Darren were both more than capable of supporting themselves in the event of a divorce and would have no need for any assistance from the other (absent an unforeseeable change in circumstances).

If a waiver of spousal support is not appropriate in your case, then you may want to consider specifying a dollar amount that either you or your spouse will owe to the other in the event of a divorce. This dollar amount may or may not be tied to the number of years you and your spouse will be married. For example, your prenuptial agreement could provide that you will pay your spouse $20,000 per year in spousal support for five years following your divorce. Or your prenuptial agreement could provide that your spouse will pay you $1,000 per month for two years if you are married for less than five years; $2,000 per month for four years if you are married for between five and ten years; $3,000 per month for five years if you are married for more than ten years.

Another way to specify the amount of spousal support you or your spouse will pay is to use a percentage of the wealthier spouse's income. For example, your prenuptial agreement could provide that you will pay your spouse 10% of your pre-tax earnings per year in spousal support for one out of every two years that you are married. (If you are married for ten years and you earn $50,000 at the end of your marriage, you would owe your spouse $5,000 per year in support for five years.)

Yet another way to specify the amount of spousal support is to tie it directly to the less well-off spouse's economic needs at the time of the divorce. For example, your prenuptial agreement could provide that you will cover the monthly rent of a two-bedroom apartment, as well as monthly leasing and insurance costs on a compact car, for your spouse for two years following your divorce. You could provide for caps on the expenses—for example, you could stipulate that you will only cover the first $1200 worth of rent. You could also agree that you will provide your spouse with the cash equivalent if your spouse chooses not to incur a listed expense—for example, by using public transportation instead of leasing a car.

Even if specifying an exact amount of spousal support in advance does not make sense in your case, it will still be worth your while to address the question of when one spouse will owe the other support. For example, you could provide in your prenup that neither spouse will owe the other support unless one spouse is earning at least 50% more than the other spouse. Or you could agree in your prenup that if the less well-off spouse's share of marital property amounts to $200,000 or more, the wealthier spouse will owe nothing in the way of support.

As you can see, there are an infinite number of ways in which you and your spouse-to-be can resolve the issue of spousal support. The exact terms of your agreement are entirely up to you. Feel free to include whatever provisions are appropriate in light of your particular circumstances, even if they are unusual.

EXAMPLE

When Neil proposed to Roxie, Roxie agreed to drop out of acting school in New York City to move to Oklahoma with him. Roxie told Neil that she would not want alimony per se if Neil left her for the girl from the farm next door, but she would want the opportunity to get her acting career back on track. So Neil agreed that in the event of a divorce, he would pay for Roxie to complete acting school in Manhattan. While paying for acting school is not what people usually think of as spousal support, the arrangement made sense in Neil and Roxie's case.

Sunset Clauses

For couples who view their prenuptial agreements primarily as divorce insurance, *sunset clauses* offer the opportunity to provide asset protection for a limited period of time, particularly in the early years of the marriage. The way a sunset clause works is that the prenuptial agreement remains in effect for a certain number of years—often five or ten. If the marriage stands the test of time, a sunset clause operates to terminate the provisions of a prenuptial agreement after the agreed-upon period of time has passed. Having a sunset clause in place often renders a prenuptial agreement more acceptable to the less wealthy spouse, who may otherwise view the agreement as a permanent symbol of distrust.

While sunset clauses do have a certain appeal, these clauses can be quite dangerous indeed. Former G.E. Chairman Jack Welch had a sunset clause built into his prenuptial agreement. A couple of years after the sunset clause took effect, the couple found themselves embroiled in a very nasty divorce. Mr. Welch settled the case for an undisclosed amount, which was no doubt for millions of dollars more than he would have if the divorce occurred while the prenuptial agreement was still in effect.

If you are considering a sunset clause, you would probably be far better off with simply providing for more favorable terms after a certain number of years have passed.

Example

Duncan had originally proposed a prenuptial agreement that would remain in effect for only five years. If Duncan and Eva divorced within five years, Eva would receive only a $15,000 distributive payment and no spousal support whatsoever. If Duncan and Eva divorced after five years, then Eva would get whatever she was entitled to under the divorce laws of their state. Duncan's lawyer suggested that instead of the sunset clause, more generous provisions would take effect after five years of marriage. For example, Duncan could agree that he would provide Eva with 25% of everything he earned during their marriage, plus $1,000 per month in spousal support for two years, if Duncan and Eva divorced after being married for five years or longer. This way, Duncan would continue to enjoy a certain level of asset protection and financial certainty in the event of a divorce—even after the test period for his marriage had passed.

PROVISIONS REGARDING CHANGES IN CIRCUMSTANCES

Courts are increasingly considering whether prenuptial agreements are fair at the time the marriage ends when deciding whether or not to enforce the terms. When a couple's circumstances change a great deal between the time they sign their prenuptial agreement and the time one of them files for divorce, a court may conclude that the terms of the prenup are too unfair to be enforced.

EXAMPLE

Zoe and her husband, Kirk, had agreed in advance that everything Zoe earned during the marriage would count as Zoe's separate property, while everything Kirk earned during the marriage would be divided equally between himself and Zoe in the event of a divorce. The agreement made sense at the time, since Kirk earned four times what Zoe earned, and Kirk had asked Zoe to waive her rights to spousal support in their prenup.

While Kirk's income had far exceeded Zoe's income at the time they signed their prenup, Zoe accidentally ended up making a small fortune during their marriage. (Zoe had been sporting a small purse she had crocheted herself out of gold twine when she was spotted by a buyer for Henri Bendel, who placed an order for a thousand of them on the spot. Zoe's crocheted purses soon became the must-have fall accessory for those in the know.) The income from Zoe's purse sales soon grew to the point that Kirk no longer needed to work as an insurance adjuster (a job he detested) in order to pay the bills. He quit his job and spent his days caring for Lily, the little girl that he and Zoe adopted.

Kirk loved his new life until Zoe filed for divorce. According to the terms of their prenup, Kirk was entitled to no portion of Zoe's earnings while Zoe had a claim to half the funds in his miniscule savings account. Kirk challenged the prenuptial agreement in light of the dramatic change in circumstances that had occurred since he and Zoe signed the prenup. The judge sided with Kirk and overturned the prenuptial agreement.

The fact is prenuptial agreements are usually negotiated based on unspoken expectations regarding the future circumstances of both spouses. When life takes you on a detour from that expected course—whether through the arrival of your second set of triplets or through a windfall inheritance from a great-uncle you never met—the terms of your prenuptial agreement may no longer be fair enough for a court to enforce.

There are two steps you should take to ensure that your prenuptial agreement will stand up in court even if your life changes a great deal over the years. First, try to anticipate some of life's changes in your prenuptial agreement. For example, you may want to provide that your fiancé will end up with a larger share of marital property if she ends up leaving her job to care for your children. Or you may want to agree that you will not seek spousal support from your husband if you are making 75% of his salary at the time of your divorce.

Second, revisit your prenuptial agreement frequently during your marriage to ensure that its terms still make sense in light of your changing circumstances. (See Rule #7 in Chapter Five.) This will keep you from having an outdated prenuptial agreement that does not reflect the new reality of your life.

CUSTODY AND VISITATION

Even if you and your spouse-to-be already have one or more children together, a court will not automatically enforce provisions relating to custody and visitation in your prenuptial agreement. This is because custody and visitation matters are decided according to the *best interests of the child* at the time a dispute arises—and not simply according to the agreement of the parents.

However, even though courts do not simply rubber stamp provisions in prenuptial agreements relating to the care and upbringing of children, some couples decide to address custody, visitation, and other child-related issues in their prenuptial agreements anyway, so each spouse is aware of the other spouse's expectations. For example, a couple in which one spouse-to-be is Jewish and the other is Catholic might agree that their children will be raised celebrating the major religious holidays of both faiths. Or a French woman and an American man might agree that if the marriage failed, the mother would be free to take the children and relocate to her native France. If you decide to address custody, visitation, or other child-related provisions in your prenuptial agreement, you should bear in mind that these provisions may very well be disregarded by the court in the event of a divorce if the court determines that the terms of your agreement are not in the best interests of your children.

CHILD SUPPORT

While you and your spouse-to-be can agree to almost anything in your prenuptial agreement with respect to your own financial rights, you cannot sign away or limit your children's right to financial support. Children have an absolute right to their parent's financial support until they are old enough to support themselves. In the event of a divorce (or if unmarried parents no longer wish to live together), the noncustodial parent is obligated to pay child support to the custodial parent. The amount of child support owed is normally determined according to financial guidelines established by your state. A court will only allow a parent to pay less than the guideline amount if the parent can show some very good reason for doing so. For example, a parent may be allowed to pay less than the amount specified under the guidelines if he or she is already supporting other children from a previous marriage.

You and your spouse-to-be can, however, agree to *more* child support than the amount required under your state's financial guidelines. If you know that the guideline amount of child support will not support your future child in the manner to which you would like him or her to be accustomed, you might want to specify a particular amount of child support in your prenuptial agreement. This will save you the trouble of waging a Patricia Duff-style child support battle years down the line. (Ms. Duff, the ex-wife of Revlon chairman Ron Perelman, wanted nothing short of $132,000 per month to care for their daughter. She was finally granted a mere $12,825 per month—the highest child support amount ever awarded in New York State at the time.)

Even if you do not count yourself among the *über*-rich, you might want to guarantee that your child will be appropriately provided for in the event of a divorce. One issue to consider addressing in your prenuptial agreement is private school and college tuition. (In most states, parents are not required to cover these educational expenses as part of their child support obligation unless it is warranted under the particular circumstances of the case.)

EXAMPLE

Wilson and Christa both came from working-class families and wanted to make sure that their children had a better chance at the good life than they had enjoyed. So Wilson and Christa agreed in their prenuptial agreement that they would make every effort to enable their children to attend the best schools and colleges possible. The agreement provided that in the event of a divorce, Wilson and Christa would share the costs of school tuition on a *pro rata* basis, proportionate to their respective incomes at the time. To ensure that spiraling education costs would not leave them bankrupt, Wilson and Christa further agreed to a cap on expenses—neither Wilson nor Christa would be forced to spend more than 25% of his or her pre-tax income on tuition expenses.

You should be aware that just as a court may decline to enforce provisions relating to custody and visitation, a court may completely disregard the terms of your child support agreement if it turns out that your child requires *more* child support than the amount agreed upon or if circumstances have changed such that it is no longer financially possible for the noncustodial parent to pay child support in the agreed-upon amount. This is because child support is *always* subject to upward or downward modification by the courts based on changes in circumstances. In light of this fact, most couples choose not to address the issue of child support in their prenuptial agreements.

Death Provisions

Your prenuptial agreement should specify each spouse's property rights in the event of the other spouse's death. Many couples choose simply to leave their entire estates to one another in the event of their death. This approach tends to work best for couples who have never been married before and who have no obligations to support children from a previous marriage or aging parents.

When people have children from a prior marriage or other objectives they wish to fulfill through their wills (such as granting a sizeable bequest to a beloved alma mater or a favorite charity), leaving all or even a majority of their estates to their soon-to-be spouses is neither possible nor desirable. A prenuptial agreement serves two purposes in these cases. First, a prenuptial agreement lets your spouse-to-be know of your estate planning goals so he or she is not unpleasantly surprised with the news after you have passed away. Second, a prenuptial agreement can include a written waiver of your soon-to-be-spouse's right to an elective share of your estate. Without a written waiver of the elective share, your spouse-to-be could frustrate your estate planning objectives by overriding the terms of your will and claiming a sizeable portion of your estate.

Your prenuptial agreement could, of course, provide for different death benefits for your surviving spouse depending on the length of your marriage.

Example

Bernard married Josie, his buxom beloved, when he was the ripe old age of 72 and she had just turned 24. Bernard believed in his heart of hearts that Josie was more interested in his *mojo* than his money (which ran into the millions of dollars), but he heeded his lawyer's advice and asked Josie to sign a prenuptial agreement. Josie agreed to waive her rights to an elective share of Bernard's estate in return for the following—at least $250,000 if Bernard died during their first three years of marriage; at least $500,000 if Bernard died after they had been married for three to seven years; and at least $1,000,000 if Bernard died after they had been married for more than seven years. (The prenup left Bernard with the flexibility to redraft his will to leave even more of his estate to Josie, if he so desired.)

Money Management Provisions

While many people limit their prenuptial agreements to divorce and death-related provisions, it is a wise idea to use your prenuptial agreement to address how you and your spouse will handle your money and other assets *during* your marriage. Your prenuptial agreement can specify:

- ◆ whether you and your spouse will maintain separate or joint bank accounts during your marriage;
- ◆ who will be responsible for joint expenses, such as your cable bill and your rent;
- ◆ how spending decisions, such as deciding whether to buy a new car, will be made during your marriage;
- ◆ how investment decisions—like deciding whether to invest in mutual funds or real estate—will be made during your marriage; and,
- ◆ what percentage of your income you will save and what percentage of your income you will spend.

Even if you and your spouse-to-be ultimately decide not to spell out your money management plan in your prenuptial agreement, discussing these issues in advance of your wedding in the context of a prenup is a tremendously valuable exercise in and of itself.

EXAMPLE
Nicole had always assumed that she and her future husband would pool their funds and maintain joint checking and savings accounts, just as her parents had done. Her fiancé, Hudson, expected that he and Nicole would continue to maintain their

own separate bank accounts after they married. The idea of keeping his own bank account gave him a reassuring sense of independence. He was certain that Nicole would feel the same way. Nicole and Hudson would probably have leapt headfirst into matrimony without realizing this important philosophical difference had it not been for a friend's suggestion that they see a financial planner before walking down the aisle. Both Nicole and Hudson agreed that it made sense to talk about money matters before starting their new life together.

The financial planner asked Nicole and Hudson each to explain their philosophy on money and how they expected that money would be handled during their marriage. Nicole went first. She told the financial planner, quite matter-of-factly, that she and Hudson were going to put all of their money into joint accounts the moment they returned from their honeymoon, and that their first order of business was to save at least $1,500 each month for a sprawling new home in the suburbs. Hudson's jaw nearly dropped to the floor. This was the first he was hearing of joint accounts, let alone saving for a home in the dreaded 'burbs. (Hudson had always fancied himself somewhat of a city slicker.) When it was his turn to speak, Hudson told the financial planner that he planned to keep his accounts in his name only during their marriage. He said that he would be happy to pay half of all of their living expenses—or even more—if it turned out that he ended up earning much more than Nicole. Hudson also said that he was not ready to begin saving for a home in the suburbs with Nicole. He wanted to be free to spend his money as he pleased during his marriage, especially in the early years before they had children.

Nicole felt incredibly hurt by everything Hudson said. It seemed as if Hudson did not trust her and did not want to share what he had with her. Hudson, on the other hand, felt that

Nicole was asking for too much too soon. His parents had been through a very nasty divorce when he was in grade school and Hudson wanted to make sure that his marriage had a strong foundation before he took important financial steps, such as merging accounts or buying a house with Nicole. Things were so shaky in their relationship after their first meeting with the financial planner that Nicole went so far as to call off the wedding, informing Hudson that she did not think he was ready for the commitment of marriage. When Nicole and Hudson finally sat down to talk, they reaffirmed their commitment to be together and decided that they had to come up with a workable financial plan.

With the assistance of a financial planner and two sets of lawyers, Hudson and Nicole entered into a prenuptial agreement providing that everything that they each earned during their marriage would count as their separate property in the event of a divorce. This provision set Hudson's mind at ease, and made him much more comfortable with the idea of merging accounts and buying real estate together with Nicole. The couple also agreed that they would each deposit half of their paychecks into a separate account in their name only and the other half into a joint account. The joint account would be used to pay living expenses and to build up enough savings for a down payment on a house someday down the line. Finally, the agreement provided that they would each maintain separate credit cards and that neither would be responsible for the other's credit card or other consumer debt.

DEBT PROVISIONS

The importance of addressing debt-related issues in advance of your marriage, whether or not you choose to do so through a prenuptial agreement, cannot be overstated. You should seriously consider specifying who will be responsible for your respective debts and other liabilities in your prenuptial agreement if:

- ◆ your spouse-to-be has a sizeable amount of credit card debt or other liabilities (such as student loans) coming into the marriage;
- ◆ you expect to incur significant debt during your marriage (for example, you plan to start a small business together using your savings, as well as loans from family members);
- ◆ your spouse-to-be is in a high-liability profession; or,
- ◆ your spouse-to-be is self-employed and you are concerned that he or she may be underreporting income for tax purposes.

You can also use a prenuptial agreement to set forth how your assets will be managed during your marriage to keep them safe from your soon-to-be spouse's creditors.

EXAMPLE

Megan was always the most well-coiffed of all of her friends. She was also the most heavily indebted, and could barely manage to pay off the minimum amount each month. Her boyfriend, Cruz, was just as much of a mall rat as Megan. He was the only man Megan had ever met who regularly tore out pages from *GQ* of clothes that he considered *must haves*. While Cruz had a wallet full of plastic, he was careful to spend only what he could afford. He paid his credit card bills in full and on time each and every month.

After Cruz popped the big question during an afternoon trip to the Donna Karan outlet, he suggested that he and Megan discuss money matters before they began planning the big day. The two exchanged their credit reports while sipping lattes at a nearby Starbucks later that month. Cruz was flabbergasted to see how much debt Megan had managed to accumulate—she earned only $48,000 a year, yet owed $32,000 in credit card debt.

Megan knew that she owed a great deal, but did not quite realize how long it was going to take her to dig herself out of the hole until Cruz ran the numbers for her.

Cruz loved Megan with all of his heart—she was his soul mate and his shopping buddy—but he wanted no part of Megan's debt. He asked her to sign a prenup providing that he would have no responsibility whatsoever for Megan's premarital debt. Their prenuptial agreement further provided that they would each maintain separate credit cards during their marriage and that neither of them would be responsible for the other's credit card debt in the event of a divorce. Finally, the prenup established that Cruz would keep his earnings and savings in a separate account in his name only. This way, Cruz's assets would be safe from Megan's creditors.

Megan's money discussions with Cruz were exactly the wake-up call Megan needed to get her financial life straightened out. After she signed the prenuptial agreement, she went to see a debt counselor to talk about restructuring her credit card liabilities and building a positive net worth.

Insurance Provisions

A prenuptial agreement can be a useful springboard for discussing the issues of life, disability, health and long-term care insurance with your soon-to-be spouse. If you and your loved one can reach agreement on these matters, you might want to set forth your understanding in your prenup.

LIFE INSURANCE

Particularly if you plan to have children or if one of you will be financially dependent on the other, you and your spouse should be certain to discuss the issue of life insurance. Life insurance is an invaluable tool to protect your loved ones in the event that one of you dies unexpectedly. The proceeds of a life insurance policy can help ensure that your loved ones can maintain their standard of living and continue pursuing their dreams (such as attending private school or going to a pricey college) in the unfortunate event that you die prematurely.

EXAMPLE

Nancy and her soon-to-be-husband, Kevin, had just purchased a beautiful six-bedroom house overlooking the lake. The house cost much more than either of them had intended to spend, and they had just barely qualified for the mortgage. Still, they had both fallen in love with the house the moment they laid eyes on it, and knew that there was no other place they would rather raise a family.

When Nancy and Kevin began talking about a prenuptial agreement, Nancy decided this was the right time to raise the issue of insurance coverage. Neither she nor Kevin would be able to afford the mortgage payment and real estate taxes on their own, and Nancy worried about the possibility that she would have to sell their beloved home—and give up all of their dreams and memories—in the event that Kevin died while he was still young. It did not take much discussion for Kevin and Nancy to agree that they would purchase two life insurance policies, one covering Kevin's life and one covering Nancy's life, in the amount necessary to enable the other to pay off the mortgage on the house and keep up with the tax payments.

One of the other advantages of life insurance is that it provides an opportunity for one spouse to leave his or her entire estate to someone else (such as a child from a prior marriage) while still providing for the needs of the other spouse.

EXAMPLE

Charlie had three grown children and two grandchildren when he met Joanna, a woman who had managed to bake her way into his heart. (He had developed quite a weakness for her melt-in-your-mouth macaroons.) Charlie did not have much in the way of money, just a small house he once shared with his first wife and about thirty thousand dollars in a savings account.

While Charlie truly loved Joanna, he wanted to be sure that the house and his savings went straight to his children and his grandchildren when he died. At the same time, he wanted to be sure that Joanna would be left with something to remember him by, so he bought a small life insurance policy in the amount of $50,000, with the proceeds payable to Joanna. When she learned that Charlie had bought a life insurance policy for her, Joanna was more than happy to sign a prenuptial agreement waiving her rights to Charlie's estate in the event of his death. (The prenuptial agreement also required Charlie to maintain the life insurance policy by paying the premiums in full and on time for the duration of their marriage.)

DISABILITY INSURANCE

While many couples are careful to purchase life insurance, far fewer couples purchase disability insurance to provide for their needs in the event that one or both of them is unable to continue working due to a health condition or physical disability. Yet, disability insurance is just as important—if not more important—than life insurance because people are *three times* more likely to become disabled than to die during their working years. If you and your spouse-to-be will be unable to cover your living expenses without one or both of your incomes, you should be absolutely certain to purchase disability insurance so that you do not have to endure a change in your standard of living in the unfortunate event of a serious health condition or physical disability.

When shopping for a disability insurance policy, you and your spouse-to-be should look for own occupation coverage if possible. This type of disability insurance will provide you with regular payments if you are unable to perform a job in your *own occupation*, even if you are able to perform some other job in some other occupation.

HEALTH INSURANCE

Especially if you and your spouse are both self-employed or work for employers who do not offer health insurance benefits, the two of you should be certain to discuss the issue of how you will cover health care costs. Health insurance premiums can be extraordinarily expensive without employer subsidization. Moreover, out-of-pocket health care costs even for insured individuals are skyrocketing. To ensure that you and your spouse-to-be can afford quality medical care at every phase of your lives together, you should come up with a plan to pay for your health care costs during your marriage. If you and your beloved are both freelance writers, for example, you might decide that one of you will work part-time as a reporter for a magazine just to qualify you both for employer-subsidized health insurance.

LONG-TERM CARE INSURANCE

While long-term care insurance is not always critical for couples in their twenties, older soon-to-be newlyweds should give some thought to long-term care insurance to protect themselves in the event that one or both spouses requires the assistance of a home health aide or full-time nursing home care. (These costs are not normally covered by standard health insurance or Medicare.) Long-term care insurance is perhaps most important for couples of moderate income, who have too much in the way of assets to qualify for Medicaid coverage but too little to cover nursing home and other long-term care costs (which can easily exceed $50,000 per year).

Norman and his sweetheart, Rita, were busy planning their wedding when a friend suggested they look into long-term care insurance. Both Norman and Rita were fit as fiddles and had no health problems of which they were aware. Still, they realized that if one of them became seriously ill and needed long-term care of any kind, the other would be left with almost nothing to live on. They talked with a financial planner and confirmed what they already knew—they were too wealthy for Medicaid and too poor to foot long-term care costs on their own. So they forked over quite a pretty penny to buy long-term care insurance for each of them. Though Norman and Rita have less spending money thanks to the hefty premiums, they both sleep better at night knowing they will be protected in the event that unexpected health problems interfere with their plans to live life to the very fullest.

Lifestyle and Other Miscellaneous Provisions

It can be tempting to turn your prenuptial agreement into a complete blueprint for your marriage, using it to cover everything from who does the dishes to how often you have to see your in-laws. Perhaps the most famous prenup in this category belongs to Rex and Teresa LeGalley. Their much publicized 1995 prenuptial agreement runs to sixteen single-spaced pages, and addresses what kind of gas they will buy (Chevron unleaded) and the frequency of healthy sex (three to five times per week).

While discussing these issues before tying the knot may help to forestall future arguments, a prenuptial agreement is really not the place to hammer out the day-to-day details of your married life. Courts will generally not enforce *lifestyle* provisions in a prenuptial agreement because courts have no interest in getting involved in the nitty-gritty of people's personal lives. The best thing to do is to stick to financial and legal issues in your prenuptial agreement. Save the laundry schedule for your refrigerator door.

7

Putting It all Together:
A Sample Prenuptial Agreement

Now that you have a good understanding of what goes into a prenup and how prenups can be negotiated, taking a closer look at a prenuptial agreement can help put it all together. This chapter looks at the prenuptial agreement entered into by Zack Mitchell and Skye Johnson, a *real life* couple from New York.

An Introduction to Zack and Skye

Zack and Skye were the type of people that always stood out at parties. Zack towered over Skye, measuring in at six feet, four inches. He had a dimple in his right cheek and laughed easily and heartily. Skye had pin-straight hair that fell down to her shoulders. She wore short skirts and heels, but somehow managed never to look provocative. Skye made her living as a real estate broker, selling high-rise condominiums in the $1,000,000 to $3,000,000 range. Zack was an executive in the music industry. The perks of his glamorous job included meeting celebrities and lunching at the hottest spots in town.

Zack had a little boy, Emilio, who was born when Zack was in his last year of college. (Emilio was the result of a summer fling with Anna, a green-eyed beauty who served him an unforgettable cup of espresso one sunny morning. One thing led to another, and Zack soon found himself saddled with the obligations but also blessed with the joys of parenthood.) Emilio was 6 years old and the apple of his father's eye. Zack was extraordinarily diligent about paying child support and spent every other weekend and at least two evenings a week enjoying time with Emilio.

Skye had never been in a serious relationship before, much less on the verge of marriage. She liked to go out on the town and live life to its fullest, but she was—in her heart of hearts—a truly traditional girl. Skye imagined a life with Zack that included lots of children (at least three) and a house with a big backyard. She was willing to follow Zack to the ends of the earth if it would help his career, because she expected that one day she would take a step back in her own career to devote herself to the demands of motherhood.

When Zack received a job offer from the Los Angeles offices of a major record label, Zack knew that it was time to take things to the next level in his relationship with Skye. He bought an emerald cut diamond ring from Tiffany's and kneeled down on one knee, trembling as he asked Skye to be his love and companion for the rest of his life. Skye accepted his proposal with tears in her eyes. It was all exactly as she had imagined.

The next morning, Skye realized that moving to Los Angeles would mean leaving behind her reputation as one of Manhattan's top real estate brokers and starting anew in an unfamiliar market. She decided to ask Zack for a prenuptial agreement, to ensure that she would be protected financially in the event the marriage ever turned sour. Skye wanted more than anything to have a family with Zack and to build a life together with him. But at the same time, she wanted to know that she would be appropriately compensated for her career sacrifices if life did not work out exactly as she had planned.

Zack was a bit taken aback when Skye suggested that they consider a prenuptial agreement. Because having a prenuptial agreement was really important to Skye, however, Zack went to see a lawyer. Zack's lawyer pointed out that Zack should be just as interested in having a prenuptial agreement as Skye. His lawyer advised him to ask Skye to waive her elective share of his estate in their prenuptial agreement, to ensure that Emilio would be well provided for even if Zack died prematurely. Zack's lawyer explained to him that prenuptial agreements were no longer simply for the rich and famous. Everyday people like Zack and Skye also stand to benefit a great deal by spelling out their financial and legal rights before walking down the aisle.

Zack and Skye's Financial Disclosure

Zack and Skye learned that before they could even begin the process of negotiating the terms of their prenuptial agreement, they would have to exchange statements of net worth setting forth their income, assets, and liabilities. While the two had discussed financial issues before on a few different occasions, they had never provided one another with the nitty-gritty details of their financial circumstances.

To organize the information they exchanged, Zack created a comparison chart of their respective financial situations.

Zack's Statement of Net Worth	Skye's Statement of Net Worth
Income	
Zack's current income is $135,000 per year. He also receives an annual bonus that is dependent on market conditions. The previous year, Zack received a bonus of $32,000, bringing his total compensation to $167,000 that year.	Skye works for a real estate brokerage firm, but she has no base salary. All of Skye's income comes in the form of real estate commissions—she earns 3% of the sale price of every high-rise condominium she sells.
Zack's income at his new job in Los Angeles would be $155,000 per year. He would also receive a signing bonus of $30,000 and would be eligible for an annual performance-based bonus of up to $25,000.	Because Skye deals exclusively with high-rise condominiums in the $1,000,000 to $3,000,000 range, she makes a great deal of money every time she makes a sale.

Zack's Net Worth
(continued)

In addition to Zack's cash compensation, he would receive approximately $30,000 worth of stock options each year at his new job in Los Angeles. These options would not vest for five years.

Zack's total annual income at his new position in Los Angeles—when taking the value of the stock options into account—would amount to $210,000 per year (assuming he received the full bonus of $25,000).

Skye's Net Worth
(continued)

In the previous year, Skye had managed to sell nine condominiums. Her total commissions amounted to $460,000.

Assets

Zack has a 401(k) plan with a current value of approximately $120,000. He also has two brokerage accounts, with a total value of approximately $300,000.

Skye owns a high-rise condominium, with a value of $1,200,000. She has nearly half a million dollars worth of equity in the condominium.

Zack does not own any real estate or other significant assets.

Skye also has a money market account in the amount of $300,000.

Liabilities

Zack has student loan debt of approximately $22,000. He also has $8,000 in credit card debt.

Skye has an outstanding mortgage of approximately $430,000. (Her high-rise condominium has appreciated in value substantially since she purchased it.)

Zack's Net Worth	Skye's Net Worth
(continued)	*(continued)*

<table>
<tr><td></td><td>She has also managed to amass nearly $43,000 in credit card debt, thanks to her frequent Madison Avenue shopping trips. (Skye always feels that she is better able to close real estate deals when she is wearing Armani and the latest pair of Manolos.)</td></tr>
</table>

Support Obligations

Zack has always been extraordinarily generous towards his son, Emilio. He pays $1,500 per month in child support to Emilio's mother, Anna. In addition, Zack pays for Emilio's educational expenses and extra-curricular activities on an as-needed basis. Last year, Zack paid $10,000 for Catholic school tuition and $1,500 for summer camp, over and above his basic child support obligation.	Skye has no support obligations.

Net Worth

All told, Zack has a net worth of $392,063.25.	Skye has a net worth of $767,342.03.

As is often the case, Zack and Skye were truly surprised to learn the details of one another's finances. Skye was shocked to learn that she had made more than double what Zack had earned in the prior year. Because of Zack's flashy lifestyle (much of which came from the perks of working for a record label), Skye had always assumed that Zack made close to half a million dollars. (Neither Zack nor Skye had ever talked about the exact numbers in the course of their financial discussions.) Skye was also somewhat taken aback by just how much Zack spent supporting his son, Emilio. Zack, on the other hand, was blown away by Skye's earnings as a real estate broker. He had no idea that Skye's lunchtime socializing and condominium showings scheduled between spa appointments were resulting in enormous real estate commissions. He was also stunned to see just how much Skye had managed to sock away.

Once Skye and Zack saw each other's statements of net worth, they both realized that it would not make much financial sense to leave behind Skye's lucrative real estate practice and move to Los Angeles, unless Zack expected substantial increases in his income. Skye's objectives for their prenuptial agreement also changed. While she had initially proposed a prenup so that she would be guaranteed an equal share of Zack's earnings in the event of a divorce, her new goal was to ensure that her premarital assets—including her high-rise condominium—would not be divided with Zack in the event of a divorce.

The Terms of Zack and Skye's Prenuptial Agreement

After a number of late night heart-to-hearts and some back and forth with their lawyers, Zack and Skye came to an agreement on the essential terms of their prenuptial agreement. Their prenuptial agreement addressed their rights regarding debts, divorce, and death—and even touched on how their money would be managed during their marriage. Zack and Skye's prenup provided as follows.

In the event of divorce. Zack and Skye agreed that they wanted their marriage to be an equal partnership, even if one of them contributed more financially. The two therefore agreed that everything they both earned during their marriage would be divided equally in the event of a divorce. There were two exceptions to this, however. Zack and Skye agreed that their pensions and other retirement benefits—including Zack's 401(k) plan—would not be divided in the event of a divorce. The couple also agreed that any stock options earned by either of them would be off-limits. (Zack's lawyer had advised him that this would be wise, as it would enable Zack to avoid the messy process of valuing and dividing unexercised stock options as part of the process of marital property division.)

Zack and Skye's prenuptial agreement further provided that all the property they each owned before their marriage—including Skye's luxury condominium and her money market account—would be considered separate property if they ever divorced, even if Zack and Skye used Skye's condominium as their marital home during their marriage. In addition, any appreciation of or income received from premarital property would be considered separate property. So if Skye rented out her condominium during their marriage, Skye's rent profits would not be counted as marital property in the event of a divorce. Similarly, if the value of Zack's brokerage accounts increased fourfold during their marriage, that increase in value would not be considered marital property.

The couple also addressed the issue of spousal support in their prenup. Even though Skye was earning so much more than Zack at the time they signed their agreement, Skye wanted to have some provisions for support in place so that she would be protected in the event that she ended up making career sacrifices to raise children. Zack was equally concerned that he might give up opportunities in his own career (for example, by deciding not to pursue the opportunity in Los Angeles) and become dependent on Skye's earnings to maintain his lifestyle. The couple agreed that if one spouse were making at least 50% more than the other spouse at the time one of them filed for divorce, the wealthier spouse would provide the other with one year of support for every two years of marriage. (If they were both earning roughly the same amount, or if one spouse were only earning 25% more than the other spouse, neither would owe the other any spousal support.)

Zack and Skye also included a formula for calculating spousal support in their prenuptial agreement. The less wealthy spouse would receive 10% of the difference between their incomes at the time of their divorce. For example, if Skye were making $50,000 while Zack were making $200,000, Skye would receive $15,000 in spousal support per year.

([Zack's gross income of $200,000 minus Skye's gross income of $50,000 = $150,000] x 10% = $15,000.)

The couple agreed that this amount would not be taxable to the less wealthy spouse.

In the event of death. Hammering out the details of their property rights in the event of death turned out to be a bit trickier than either Zack or Skye had anticipated. Zack's primary concern was ensuring that his son, Emilio, be well provided for in the event of his death. To protect Emilio, Zack asked Skye to waive her elective share of his estate so that he would have the freedom to leave the majority of his estate to Emilio if he so chose. Zack also asked Skye to waive her beneficiary rights to his 401(k) plan.

While Skye understood Zack's desire to provide as much as possible for Emilio if he died prematurely, she was hurt that Zack was only focused on providing for Emilio and did not seem to be giving much thought to providing for her. Skye wanted to make sure that she, too, would be adequately protected in the event of Zack's death. She also worried about what would happen if she and Zack had children together during their marriage. If Zack left almost everything to Emilio, what would be left for the children that she and Zack had together?

It took quite a few discussions before Zack and Skye were able to reach agreement on the inheritance-related provisions of their prenuptial agreement. The two finally agreed that in the event of one spouse's death, the other spouse would be entitled to any jointly-titled marital home as well as all the funds in their joint checking, savings, and brokerage accounts. This meant that if Zack died, Skye would not have to turn over their home or any of the money in their joint accounts to Emilio. Each spouse would be free to dispose of the remainder of his or her estate—including premarital property and pensions—in whatever manner he or she pleased. This provision gave Zack the flexibility to designate Emilio as the beneficiary of his 401(k).

To ensure that there would be enough left over to provide for any children that Zack and Skye had together, the couple agreed that they would purchase two, $250,000 life insurance policies—one insuring each of their lives—for the benefit of *each* of the children they had together. For example, if Zack and Skye had two children together, the agreement required that they purchase *four* $250,000 life insurance policies—one policy insuring each of their lives for each child. This would ensure that each child would receive $250,000 in life insurance proceeds if either Zack or Skye died. Skye was much more comfortable with the terms of their prenuptial agreement because of this life insurance provision. She felt she no longer had to worry that Emilio's inheritance would take away from her own children's inheritances or that there would not be enough assets to go around in the event of Zack's death. The agreement ensured that each of her children would be guaranteed a quarter of a million dollars in life insurance proceeds.

Debt provisions. Zack was a bit taken aback by the amount of credit card debt that Skye had managed to rack up. (He had always thought she was quite a natty dresser, but had no idea just how much her Imelda Marcos-style shoe collection had been costing her.) While he himself had credit card debt, his own debt was incurred for living expenses while he was in school—not shopping trips on Madison

Avenue. Zack was worried that Skye would continue spending herself silly, particularly once she had access to his income as well as her own. Skye, for her part, wanted to ensure that she would not be held liable for Zack's student loan debt after they were married. (Even though Zack's student loan debt was not nearly as large as some people's debt burdens, Skye felt that—as a matter of principle—she should not be responsible for Zack's schooling costs.)

After some discussion, the two decided that it would be best if they each wiped their financial slates clean (using premarital assets) prior to tying the knot, so that they could begin married life debt-free. This meant that Zack had to borrow against his 401(k) to pay off his student loan and credit card debt, while Skye had to take out a home equity loan to clear her tabs at the city's chicest department stores.

Money management during the marriage. Because they both felt that their marriage should be an equal economic partnership, Zack and Skye agreed that they would deposit all of their earnings during their marriage into a joint checking account. The funds in this account would be used to pay all of their living expenses—such as rent or mortgage payments, grocery and dining out bills, and utility costs. The couple also agreed that if they decided to live in Skye's condominium during their marriage, they would pay only 50% of the mortgage payments on the condominium out of their joint checking account. Skye would be responsible to pay the remaining 50% using her separate property funds. (This arrangement was only fair, since Skye did not want any part of her condominium to be considered marital property in the event of a divorce.)

Both Zack and Skye felt that they should save and invest as much as possible. Therefore they agreed that they would save a minimum of 10% of their combined income, and that this money would be invested only in mutual funds pegged to the major stock indices (such as the Vanguard 500 Index Fund) in a discount brokerage account. (Zack wanted to specify in advance the type of investments they would make with their savings to prevent any disagreement over the risk level or other aspects of their investment strategy at a later time.)

The couple also wanted to be fiscally responsible when it came time for them to purchase their first home together. Zack and Skye specified in their prenup that they would not purchase a home for an amount in excess of three times their combined income. They also agreed that in the event of a divorce, the home would be immediately sold (even if the couple had children by that time) and the proceeds would be divided equally between them.

Zack and Skye also addressed spending-related issues in their prenuptial agreement. The first of these issues was child support for Emilio. While Skye was very fond of Emilio, she wanted to have some limits in place as to how much money Zack could spend on Emilio. She had no problem with the amount that Zack was currently spending on Emilio, but she did not want it to balloon to an unreasonable sum over the years. Zack understood Skye's concerns, and agreed that he would not spend more than $24,000 per year from their joint account on Emilio. However, Zack would be free to use the funds in his brokerage account or other separate property for Emilio's benefit.

Just as Skye was concerned that Zack would spend an excessive sum on Emilio, Zack was nervous about the shopaholic syndrome from which Skye was apparently suffering. Zack initially proposed that Skye receive a shopping budget of $15,000 per year, that she could use any way she pleased. Skye balked at Zack's suggestion. Since she made so much more than Zack, why should she have such stringent limits on her spending? Zack finally agreed that Skye should be allowed to spend up to $24,000 per year on shopping using the funds in their joint account—the exact same amount that Zack was allowed to spend on Emilio. He thought the agreement was a tad unfair, since Emilio's care was a necessity while shopping was a frivolity. But he understood Skye's point about the disparity in their earnings and decided it was a workable arrangement.

Lastly, the couple decided to provide in their prenuptial agreement that they would share responsibility for any debts incurred during their marriage for living expenses. If Skye rung up a giant bill at Barneys over and above her allotted $24,000 shopping budget, however, she would be solely responsible for that debt. In the same way, Zack would be responsible for any debt incurred for the support of Emilio (over and above his allotted $24,000 from their joint funds). The couple agreed to open a joint credit card account to pay all joint living expenses (such as grocery and travel bills). They further agreed that the credit card bill would be paid off in full each month. To provide each of them with some measure of financial freedom during their marriage, they also agreed that they would maintain their separate credit cards as well. The bills from these credit cards would be paid off using separate property, and neither would be responsible for the other's separate debt. Finally, to ensure that their joint credit card account would not be abused, Zack and Skye also provided in their prenuptial agreement that they would each have to consult with the other before making any purchase in excess of $1,000.

Other miscellaneous provisions. Fortunately, neither Zack nor Skye had any interest in spelling out true lifestyle-related provisions in their prenuptial agreement (such as who does the dishes on Thursday nights). The only noneconomic provision included in the prenuptial agreement was that the couple expected their children to be raised with a healthy respect for all religions, but without any formal adherence to any particular religion. Skye insisted on this provision because she did not want Zack's mother—who attended Sunday Mass even during the biggest snowstorms of the year—to force the couple to raise their children as practicing Roman Catholics.

The Final Document:
Zack and Skye's Prenuptial Agreement

Once Zack and Skye had reached agreement on the terms of their prenuptial agreement, Zack's lawyer prepared a first draft of the agreement. Skye's lawyer then *marked up* the agreement with her comments. After some back and forth, the agreement was finalized. Zack and Skye signed their agreement three months in advance of their wedding, before their invitations had even been sent out. Their wedding took place on a glorious spring day—just as Skye had envisioned—and Emilio made quite a handsome ring bearer.

Zack and Skye's prenuptial agreement is set forth below, with notes in the margins explaining why the agreement is structured the way that it is.

PRENUPTIAL AGREEMENT

AGREEMENT made this 19th day of November 2004 by and between Zachary Michael Mitchell ("Zack"), residing at 14 Willoughby Street, Apt. 2E, New York, New York 10023 and Skye Ann Johnson ("Skye"), residing at 25 Riverside Avenue, Apt. 4F, New York, New York 10021.

W I T N E S S E T H

WHEREAS, Zack and Skye intend to marry;

WHEREAS, neither Zack nor Skye has been previously married;

WHEREAS, Zack has one child, Emilio Stephan Mitchell ("Emilio"), born on June 14, 1998;

WHEREAS, Skye has no children;

The first order of business in a prenuptial agreement is to set forth the names of the parties and the date of the agreement. Instead of repeating the full name of each person throughout the agreement, the agreement will usually specify a short name (such as Zack and Skye) for each spouse-to-be.

WHEREAS, Zack and Skye have each made full and fair disclosure to the other of his or her financial worth and all circumstances relevant to his or her current or future financial situation;

WHEREAS Zack and Skye each acknowledges that he or she is entering into this Agreement of his or her own accord, after consultation with independent counsel of his or her own choosing;

WHEREAS, Zack and Skye intend that their respective property rights and obligations during the marriage, in the event of a divorce or dissolution of the marriage, or the death of one of the parties, shall be established and governed solely by this Agreement;

WHEREAS, Zack and Skye desire by this Agreement to establish certain property as Separate Property, which each party shall be free to manage or dispose of in any way he or she pleases both during the marriage and in the event of either party's death;

WHEREAS, Zack and Skye further desire that each party's Separate Property shall not be divided in the event of a divorce;

WHEREAS, Zack and Skye desire by this Agreement to establish an equal economic partnership during their marriage; and,

WHEREAS, Zack and Skye further desire by this Agreement to establish certain property as Marital Property, which shall be shared equally between the parties during the marriage and in the event that their marriage ends in divorce;

NOW, THEREFORE, in consideration of the upcoming marriage of the parties and the promises and undertakings contained herein, Zack and Skye do mutually agree as follows:

I. General Statement of Intentions

Zack and Skye plan to marry one another in the near future and desire by this Agreement to establish their economic rights and obligations with respect to one another during the marriage, in the event of a divorce or dissolution of the marriage, and in the event of the death of one of the parties.

Many prenups begin with a general statement explaining the purpose and intention of the agreement.

II. Governing Law

Zack and Skye acknowledge and agree that, no matter where they reside in the future, all of their economic obligations and rights with respect to one another during the marriage, in the event of a divorce or dissolution of the marriage, or the death of one of the parties, shall be governed solely by this Agreement.

This provision ensures that the terms of Zack and Skye's prenuptial agreement will remain in effect even if they move to another state, with different divorce and inheritance laws.

Every prenuptial agreement should specify which state's law will govern the interpretation of the agreement in the event of a dispute. Zack and Skye chose New York, since they lived there.

Because comprehensive financial disclosure is the cornerstone of any valid prenuptial agreement, every agreement usually includes a section confirming that each person provided the other with comprehensive financial disclosure.

Zack and Skye further acknowledge and agree that no matter where they reside in the future, this Agreement shall be governed by the laws of the State of New York and no other law, including the law of community or marital property or equitable distribution of any state, shall ever apply to this Agreement or to the parties' rights hereunder.

III. Financial Disclosure

Skye declares and acknowledges that Zack has informed her of his current and expected income, the approximate value of his assets and liabilities, and any and all other facts necessary for a complete understanding of Zack's current and expected future financial circumstances. Skye further declares and acknowledges that Zack has provided her with a complete and comprehensive Statement of Net Worth, annexed hereto as Exhibit A.

Zack declares and acknowledges that Skye has informed him of her current and expected income, the approximate value of her assets and liabilities, and any and all other facts necessary for a complete understanding of Skye's current and expected future financial circumstances. Zack further declares and acknowledges that Skye has provided her with a complete and comprehensive Statement of Net Worth, annexed hereto as Exhibit B.

Zack warrants and represents to Skye that he has provided her with complete and accurate financial information regarding any and all other facts necessary for a complete understanding of his current and expected future financial circumstances.

Skye warrants and represents to Zack that he has provided her with complete and accurate financial information regarding any and all other facts necessary for a complete understanding of her current and expected future financial circumstances.

Zack agrees and acknowledges that he has had sufficient time to review Skye's financial disclosures, has had any questions satisfactorily answered by Skye, and accordingly has a thorough understanding of Skye's current and expected future financial circumstances.

Skye agrees and acknowledges that she has had sufficient time to review Zack's financial disclosures, has had any questions satisfactorily answered by Zack, and accordingly has a thorough understanding of Zack's current and expected future financial circumstances.

IV. Advice of Counsel

Zack agrees and acknowledges that he consulted with independent and well-qualified counsel of his own choosing prior to executing this Agreement. Zack acknowledges that he was represented by Anna Kraus, Esq., a matrimonial lawyer with the firm of Thacher & Wardwell, 425 Madison Avenue, New York, New York 10017.

Courts are much more likely to uphold prenuptial agreements entered into after both parties had the opportunity to consult with independent counsel of their own choosing. Accordingly, prenuptial agreements generally specify the name of each party's lawyer and contain an acknowledgement by each party that he or she received appropriate legal advice prior to signing the agreement.

Skye agrees and acknowledges that she consulted with independent and well-qualified counsel of her own choosing prior to executing this Agreement. Skye acknowledges that she was represented by Nina Cohen, Esq., a matrimonial lawyer with the firm of Shearman & Skadden, 803 Third Avenue, New York, New York 10012.

Both Zack and Skye agree and acknowledge that they have each been informed by their respective counsel of their legal rights arising from their upcoming marriage in the property currently owned by each of them and any property acquired by either or both of them during their marriage, both during the marriage and in the event of a dissolution of their marriage by death, divorce or any other means. They each acknowledge that they enter into this Agreement with full knowledge of these rights and desire nevertheless that this Agreement—rather than the domestic relations or estate and probate laws of any state—govern their property rights with respect to one another both during their marriage and in the event of a dissolution of their marriage for any reason.

V. Voluntary Execution Of Agreement

Skye agrees and acknowledges that she is entering into this Agreement freely, and of her own accord. Skye further agrees and acknowledges that she was not under duress at the time she signed the Agreement, nor coerced to sign the Agreement by any person.

This clause confirms that each person's lawyer explained the default rules on issues such as spousal support and inheritance rights to him or her.

Prenuptial agreements are often challenged on the grounds that one person was forced to sign the agreement and give up valuable property rights against his or her own will. Most lawyers therefore include a provision stating that each person entered into the agreement voluntarily, without any undue pressure from the other party.

Zack agrees and acknowledges that he is entering into this Agreement freely, and of his own accord. Zack further agrees and acknowledges that he was not under duress at the time he signed the Agreement, nor coerced to sign the Agreement by any person.

VI. Consideration

Zack and Skye each acknowledge that he or she would not enter into their contemplated marriage, except for the execution of this Agreement.

This section is pure legalese. It just provides that the parties would not proceed with their planned marriage without having their prenuptial agreement in place.

VII. Separate Property

For the purposes of this Agreement, the term "Separate Property" means:

This section defines certain categories of property as Separate Property that is off limits and will not be divided in the event of a divorce.

All property owned by either party prior to the marriage, including but not limited to the property identified on Zack's Statement of Net Worth (annexed hereto as Exhibit A) and Skye's Statement of Net Worth (annexed hereto as Exhibit B);

Any and all pensions and other retirement benefits owned by or due to either party, regardless of whether such pension or other retirement benefit is earned or accrued before or after the marriage;

Zack and Skye agreed that pensions, retirement benefits, and stock options would count as separate property.

Any and all stock options owned by or due to either party, regardless of whether such stock options are earned or acquired before or during the marriage; and,

Zack and Skye decided that any property either of them received during their marriage by way of gift or inheritance would be considered their respective separate property.

These clauses confirm that the appreciation of and income from separate property will also considered separate property.

This clause confirms that if some separate property asset is sold, the proceeds will count as separate property.

Because New York courts consider enhanced earning capacity (such as the potential earnings increase from getting a medical degree) to be a marital asset subject to division in a divorce, Zack and Skye specifically waived their rights to the other's enhanced earning capacity and professional goodwill.

Any gifts or inheritances received by either party (whether by bequest, devise, or descent), regardless of whether such gifts or inheritances were acquired before or during the marriage.

The term "Separate Property" shall include the appreciation in the value of the property described above, whether or not due to the other party's contributions or efforts, direct or indirect, to the contributions or efforts of others, or to inflation or to market contributions.

The term "Separate Property" shall also include the rents, profits, and any and all other income from the property described above, regardless of whether such rents, profits, or income is earned or acquired before or during the marriage.

The term "Separate Property" shall also include all property acquired in exchange for a party's Separate Property and the proceeds from the sale, acquisition, or transfer of a party's Separate Property.

The term "Separate Property" shall also include the professional goodwill and/or enhanced earning capacity of either party, regardless of whether the other party contributed directly or directly to such enhanced earning capacity or professional goodwill.

Zack and Skye agree that Zack shall keep and retain sole ownership, control, and enjoyment of all Separate Property, as defined herein, including but not limited to the property identified on Zack's Statement of Net Worth (annexed hereto as Exhibit A) and any appreciation of such Separate Property or income from such Separate Property, regardless of whether such appreciation occurs or income is earned during the marriage. Skye agrees that Zack shall hold all such property free from any claim, lien, or right, inchoate or otherwise, on the part of Skye and that Zack may dispose of any part or all of such property, at any time or times and in any manner he may see fit.

Zack and Skye agree that Skye shall keep and retain sole ownership, control, and enjoyment of all Separate Property, as defined herein, including but not limited to the property identified on Skye's Statement of Net Worth (annexed hereto as Exhibit B) and any appreciation of such Separate Property or income from such Separate Property, regardless of whether such appreciation occurs or income is earned during the marriage. Zack agrees that Skye shall hold all such property free from any claim, lien, or right, inchoate or otherwise, on the part of Zack and that Skye may dispose of any part or all of such property, at any time or times and in any manner she may see fit.

These clauses establish that Zack and Skye are each free to do whatever they wish with respect to their Separate Property, and that neither has any claim of any kind to the other's Separate Property.

Because Zack and Skye wished to have retirement funds (such as 401(k) plans) be considered Separate Property, while providing that all income earned during the marriage be considered Marital Property, Zack's lawyer insisted that there be a provision establishing that each party can contribute income earned during the marriage to his or her 401(k) plan or other retirement plan without having the funds in the retirement plan be considered Marital Property.

By law, spouses are entitled to be named as the beneficiary of certain pension, retirement, and profit-sharing plans. These rights must be waived in writing after the marriage has taken place. Accordingly, this paragraph ensures that Zack and Skye will sign all documents necessary to waive their rights to one another's pension/retirement funds within a certain period of time after the marriage has taken place.

Without limiting the generality of the foregoing paragraphs, each party waives any and all state and federal rights he or she may otherwise have in any pension, retirement, or profit-sharing plan of the other party. Zack and Skye further agree that each party may contribute the maximum allowable amount to 401(k) plans and other retirement plans during the marriage and that the funds in each person's 401(k) plan and other retirement plans will nevertheless be considered Separate Property.

In the event of the death of either party, Emilio (Zack's son) is named as the beneficiary of Zack's retirement accounts and plans. As set forth on her Statement of Net Worth, annexed hereto as Exhibit B, Skye currently has no retirement accounts or related plans. Skye agrees to execute any and all acknowledgements, consents, and any other documents necessary to formalize her waiver of any interest in Zack's pension, retirement, and profit-sharing plans in accordance with the terms of this Agreement within three months of the date of their marriage. Should Skye at any point acquire a pension, retirement, or profit-sharing plan, Zack agrees to execute any and all acknowledgements, consents, and any other documents necessary to formalize his waiver of any interest in Skye's pension, retirement, and/or profit-sharing plan within three months of the date of such acquisition.

VIII. Marital Property

For the purposes of this Agreement, the term "Marital Property" means all property of any kind earned or acquired by either Zack or Skye during the marriage, with the exception of property classified as "Separate Property" above. The term "Marital Property" includes the appreciation in value of the rents, profits, and other income from; and all property acquired in exchange for the property classified as "Marital Property" above.

Zack and Skye agree that they will have equal rights to all Marital Property and that they will share ownership, control and enjoyment of all Marital Property.

IX. Commingling Of Income And Assets

The parties recognize that it is possible for their Marital Property and Separate Property to become, or appear to become, commingled. It is the parties' intention that any commingling of Marital Property or Separate Property shall not be interpreted to imply any abandonment of the terms and provisions of this Agreement, absent a written modification of this Agreement signed and acknowledged by both parties.

X. Debt

Zack and Skye acknowledge and agree that they shall each remain solely liable for their respective premarital, individual debts, including but not limited to the liabilities set forth on their respective

This section establishes that Zack and Skye wish to designate all property earned or acquired during the marriage (with the exception of property classified as Separate Property above) as Marital Property.

This section ensures that even if Separate Property is mixed with Marital Property (for example, by depositing inheritance funds into a joint account), the Separate Property will remain separate absent a written agreement providing otherwise.

This section sets forth the parties' understanding with respect to debts and liabilities. Specifically, their agreement establishes that neither party shall be liable for the other's premarital debts, but both parties shall be liable for debts incurred during the marriage in connection with living expenses and the like.

Statements of Net Worth, annexed hereto as Exhibits A and B. Both Zack and Skye agree to undertake their best efforts to pay off their respective premarital, individual debts (with the exception of mortgage loans) prior to the parties' marriage. In the event that either party is unable to pay off his or her premarital, individual debts prior to the marriage, Zack and Skye agree that Marital Property may not be used towards the payment of either party's premarital, individual debts, except as otherwise provided herein.

Zack and Skye further acknowledge and agree that they will establish joint credit card accounts to cover their living expenses during the marriage, and anticipate that they may take out joint mortgage and/or home equity loans during their marriage. The parties shall be jointly responsible for these debts.

In light of their different spending needs, Zack and Skye agreed that it would make sense to each maintain separate credit card accounts (for which they would each be solely liable) in addition to joint credit card accounts. This way, Zack could spend additional sums on Emilio's care without upsetting Skye and Skye could spend additional sums on the season's latest fashions without affecting Zack's credit rating.

Zack and Skye also agree that they will each continue to maintain separate credit card accounts during their marriage. Zack's separate credit card accounts may be used to cover expenses relating to the care and support of Zack's son, Emilio, over and above the maximum amount that may be spent using Marital Property as set forth in Section XI below. Skye's separate credit card accounts may be used to cover her personal shopping expenses over and above the maximum amount that may be spent using Marital Property as set forth in Section XI below. Zack and Skye agree and acknowledge that Zack shall remain solely liable for his separate credit card debt and Skye shall remain solely liable for her separate credit card debt.

XI. Money Management During The Marriage

Zack and Skye agree that they shall open and maintain joint checking and savings accounts (the "Joint Accounts") for the duration of their marriage. Zack and Skye each agree that all income, bonuses, or other cash compensation that he or she earns during the marriage shall be immediately deposited into the Joint Accounts.

The funds in the Joint Account shall be used to cover the parties' living expenses, including but not limited to rent, mortgage payments, grocery bills, utility bills, clothing expenses, vacation costs, and the expenses relating to any children born to or adopted by the parties. The funds in the Joint Account shall also be used to cover child support and related payments to Zack's son, Emilio, up to a maximum of $24,000 per year. Finally, the funds in the Joint Account shall be used to cover Skye's personal shopping expenses, up to a maximum of $24,000 per year. Should Zack wish to spend more than $24,000 per year for the support of his son, Emilio, Zack shall use his Separate Property funds to provide for any support in excess of $24,000. Should Skye wish to spend more than $24,000 per year on her personal shopping-related expenses, Skye shall use her Separate Property funds to cover any personal shopping-related expenses in excess of $24,000 per year.

Not all couples decide to hammer out their money management plan in a prenuptial agreement, but Zack and Skye thought that doing so would help them avoid lots of arguments down the line. In this section, Zack and Skye specify how their earnings will be handled, who will be responsible for their living expenses, and how investment decisions will be made, among other things.

Zack and Skye further agree to open and maintain one or more joint credit card accounts during the marriage (the "Joint Credit Cards"). The Joint Credit Cards shall be used to pay for the parties' living expenses during the marriage. Zack and Skye agree that the balances for the Joint Credit Cards shall be paid off in full each month, using the funds in the parties' Joint Accounts. Zack and Skye further agree to consult with one another before making any purchase in excess of $1,000 using the Joint Credit Cards.

If the parties choose to live in a residence that constitutes one parties' Separate Property (such as Skye's Manhattan condominium, identified on her Statement of Net Worth, annexed hereto as Exhibit B), the parties shall pay 50% of the mortgage, real estate taxes, and other carrying costs using the funds in the Joint Account. The party to whom the marital residence belongs shall be solely responsible for the remaining 50% of the mortgage, real estate taxes, and other carrying costs and shall pay such expenses using Separate Property. Even if the parties choose to live in a residence that constitutes one spouse's Separate Property and even if the parties use Marital Property to pay 50% of the mortgage, real estate taxes, and other carrying costs on the property during the parties' marriage, the residence shall remain Separate Property and no part of the value of the residence shall be considered Marital Property.

Zack and Skye further agree that during their marriage, they will invest no less than 10% of their combined income in mutual funds pegged to the major stock indices (such as the Vanguard 500 Index Fund) through Charles Schwab or another discount brokerage firm.

In the event that parties purchase a home together during their marriage, Zack and Skye agree that they will not purchase a home for an amount in excess of three times their combined income. Zack and Skye further agree that they will each receive a credit for any Separate Property (but not the appreciation on such Separate Property) contributed by him or her for the purchase, renovation, or improvement of a home held in the parties' joint names, and further agree that such Separate Property will be returned to the party who contributed such Separate Property in the event of the sale of the home.

This provision establishes that if Zack or Skye contributes Separate Property towards the purchase of a jointly-held home, they will each be entitled to a reimbursement of that Separate Property when the home is sold.

XII. Estate Rights

Zack hereby waives and releases all rights and interests, statutory or otherwise, including but not limited to the right to be executor of Skye's will or administrator of her estate, widower's allowance, statutory allowance, exempt property, homestead exemption, distribution in intestacy, and right of election to take against the will of Skye or against Skye's testamentary substitutes which he might acquire as Skye's husband, widower, heir-at-law, next-of-kin, or distributee, in her Separate

These clauses provide that Zack and Skye each waive their right to any elective share of the other's estate.

Property as defined herein. Except as specifically provided herein, Zack does not waive any right he may have in the parties' Marital Property as defined herein.

Skye hereby waives and releases all rights and interests, statutory or otherwise, including but not limited to the right to be executor of Zack's will or administrator of his estate, widow's allowance, statutory allowance, exempt property, homestead exemption, distribution in intestacy, and right of election to take against the will of Zack or against Zack's testamentary substitutes which she might acquire as Zack's wife, widow, heir-at-law, next-of-kin, or distributee, in his Separate Property as defined herein. Except as specifically provided herein, Skye does not waive any right she may have in the parties' Marital Property as defined herein.

This section establishes the bare minimum that each spouse is entitled to in the event that the other spouse dies—all funds in their joint accounts as well as any home held jointly by the two of them.

Zack and Skye hereby agree and acknowledge that in the event of the death of either of them, the surviving spouse shall be entitled to retain any jointly-held marital home, as well all funds in the parties' Joint Accounts.

This provision ensures that Zack and Skye can each leave more than the bare minimum to the other in his or her will.

Nothing in this Agreement shall be construed as a waiver or renunciation by either party of any bequest, devise, or gift made to him or her, as the case may be, or the naming of either party as executor or administrator of his/her estate, in the Last Will and Testament of the other or during their lifetimes, but each of the parties acknowledges that no representations or promises of any kind or nature have been made to him or her with respect to any gift, bequest, or other testamentary benefit.

XIII. Life Insurance

In the event that Zack and Skye have or adopt children together, Zack and Skye agree, *for each child*, to maintain *two* life insurance policies naming the child as the beneficiary: life insurance on Zack's life in the amount of at least $250,000 and life insurance on Skye's life in the amount of at least $250,000. These policies shall remain in effect until the child reaches age twenty-one. The premiums on these policies shall be paid using Marital Property.

This provision establishes that Zack and Skye will purchase separate life insurance policies naming each of their children as beneficiaries, so that their children are adequately provided for in the event of either parent's premature death.

XIV. Equal Division of Marital Property in the Event of a Divorce, Dissolution of Marriage, or Separation

Zack and Skye agree that upon the entry of a judgment in a marital action (unless the parties agree in a notarized writing to make such division earlier), all Marital Property—including but not limited to cash, savings, brokerage and other investment accounts, furnishings, furniture, household effects, vehicles, and boats—shall be divided equally between Zack and Skye.

Because Zack and Skye viewed their marriage as an equal economic partnership, this section provides that all Marital Property shall be divided equally between them in the event of a divorce.

Zack and Skye also agree that any residence held jointly by Zack and Skye shall be sold as soon as possible following the entry of a judgment in a marital action (unless the parties agree in a notarized

When there are children of the marriage, many courts will postpone the sale of the marital home until the children are grown up. This can cause financial difficulties for the noncustodial parent, who does not receive his or her share of the home's value until many years after the divorce. To circumvent this problem, Zack and Skye provide in their prenuptial agreement that their marital home will be sold in the event of a divorce.

This section establishes that Zack and Skye waive any interest they may each have to the other's Separate Property in the event of a divorce. This section further establishes that Zack and Skye understood the factors that New York courts would otherwise have considered when distributing the property they have decided to mark as Separate Property, and have nevertheless knowingly waived their rights to the other's Separate Property.

writing to make such a division earlier), with the proceeds to be divided equally between Zack and Skye. The parties agree and acknowledge to sell any jointly-held property in the event of a divorce, even if the parties have children together and the children have grown accustomed to living in the residence and in full knowledge of the fact that a New York court may postpone the sale of any jointly-held residence until the child(ren) of the marriage reached the age of eighteen under those circumstances.

XV. Waiver of Equitable Distribution of Separate Property in the Event of a Divorce, Dissolution of Marriage, or Separation

Zack and Skye each acknowledge that he or she has been apprised of the factors a New York court would consider when making an equitable distributive award in the context of a divorce. Factors a New York court would consider include:

a. The income and property of each party at the time of marriage and at the time of the commencement of the action;

b. The duration of the marriage and the age and health of both parties;

c. The need of a custodial parent to occupy or own the marital residence and to use or own its household effects;

d. The loss of inheritance and pension rights upon dissolution of the date of the marriage as of the date of dissolution;

e. Any award of maintenance under Domestic Relations Law § 236(B)(6);

f. Any equitable claim to, interest in, or direct or indirect contribution made to the acquisition of marital property by the party not having title, including joint efforts or expenditures and contributions as a wage earner and homemaker and to the career or career potential of the other party;

g. The liquid or nonliquid character of marital property;

h. The probable future financial circumstances of each party;

i. The impossibility or difficulty of evaluating any component asset or any interest in a business, corporation, or profession, and the economic desirability of retaining such asset or interest intact and free from any claim or interference by the other party;

j. The tax consequences to each party;

k. The wasteful dissipation of assets by either spouse;

l. Any transfer or encumbrance made in contemplation of a matrimonial action without fair consideration; and,

m. Any other factor that the court shall expressly find to be just and proper.

Both Zack and Skye acknowledge that they have considered these factors and have agreed nonetheless to waive and renounce any right to an equitable distributive award that he or she may otherwise have had with respect to the other's Separate Property.

Zack and Skye further acknowledge and agree that within ten days of the commencement of a marital action, Zack shall vacate any home (including any marital residence) owned solely by Skye at the time of the commencement of the marital action.

XVI. Spousal Support in the Event of a Divorce, Dissolution of Marriage, or Separation

Zack and Skye each acknowledge and agree that they are both talented individuals who are fully capable of supporting themselves. The parties recognize, however, that one of them may become financially dependent upon the other during the course of the marriage and that, in the event the marriage ends in divorce, the financially dependent spouse will require support in order to maintain his or her lifestyle. The parties accordingly agree as follows with respect to spousal support:

Skye was concerned about what would happen in the event that the two of them decided to live in her condominium during their marriage. This clause establishes that Zack must leave her condominium almost immediately in the event of a divorce.

This section provides for spousal support in the event that one spouse is earning substantially more the other at the time of a divorce.
To provide as much certainty as possible, this section establishes a formula for determining the amount and duration of spousal support.

If either Zack or Skye is earning 50% more than the other at the time of the commencement of an action for a divorce or legal separation, the higher-earning spouse shall pay one year of spousal support to the lower-earning spouse for every two years of the marriage, up to a maximum of four years. For example, if the marriage lasts ten years, spousal support shall be paid for no longer than four years.

Zack and Skye thought it would make sense to put a cap of four years on the duration of spousal support (so that they could move on with their lives free of any obligation to one another within a reasonable period of time in the event that their marriage ended).

The annual amount of spousal support shall be 10% of the difference between the gross, pre-tax income of the higher-earning spouse and the gross, pre-tax income of the lower-earning spouse. For example, if Skye is making $50,000 while Zack is making $200,000 at the time of the commencement of an action for a divorce or legal separation, Skye would receive $15,000 in spousal support per year.

Spousal support shall not be taxable to the recipient, nor tax deductible to the payer.

Spousal support is usually taxable to the recipient. Zack and Skye decided to provide that spousal support would not be taxable to the recipient.

The lower-earning spouse shall be entitled to spousal support the moment that either spouse commences an action for a divorce or legal separation, regardless of the jurisdiction, venue, or location of such action.

Spousal support shall terminate immediately in the event of the death of either spouse or the remarriage of the lower-earning spouse.

This clause provides that if neither spouse is earning substantially more than the other at the time of a divorce, then no spousal support shall be owed by either Zack or Skye. To be on the safe side, this section also establishes that Zack and Skye understood the factors that New York courts would otherwise have considered when awarding spousal support, and that the two have nevertheless knowingly waived their rights to spousal support except as provided under the Agreement.

Zack and Skye further agree that if neither spouse is earning 50% more than the other at the time of the commencement of an action for a divorce or legal separation, then neither spouse shall be entitled to receive maintenance, alimony or support from the other, whether temporary (i.e., during the pendency of an action for divorce or legal separation) or permanent (i.e., after the entry of a judgment in an action for divorce or legal separation).

Zack and Skye each acknowledge that he or she has been apprised of and considered the factors that a New York court would considering in making any alimony, maintenance, or support award, which factors are as follows:

a. The income and property of the respective parties, including marital property distributed pursuant to the Domestic Relations Law 236(b)(5);

b. The duration of the marriage and the age and health of both parties;

c. The present and future earning capacity of both parties;

d. The ability of the party seeking maintenance to become self-supporting and, if applicable, the period of time and training necessary therefore;

e. Reduced or lost lifetime earning capacity of the party seeking maintenance as a result of having foregone or delayed education, training, employment, or career opportunities during the marriage;

f. The presence of children of the marriage in the respective homes of the parties;

g. The tax consequences to each party;

h. Contributions and services of the party seeking maintenance as a spouse, parent, wage earner, and homemaker and to the career or career potential of the other party;

i. The wasteful dissipation of marital property by either spouse; and,

j. Any transfer or encumbrance made in contemplation of a matrimonial action without fair consideration; and any other factor which the court shall expressly find to be just and proper.

XVII. Voluntary Transfers Permissible; No Waiver

Notwithstanding any other provision of this Agreement, Zack and Skye shall each have the right voluntarily to transfer or convey to the other any property or interest therein which may be lawfully conveyed or transferred during his or her lifetime, or by will or otherwise upon death, and neither Zack nor Skye intends by this Agreement to limit or

This section provides that Zack and Skye are allowed to give one another more than what is provided for under the terms of the Agreement. For example, if Skye wished to give Zack half of her condominium by adding his name to the title, she would be free to do so. (She just would not be obligated to do so, since the condominium is her separate property.)

restrict in any way the right and power of the other to receive any such voluntary transfer or conveyance.

XVIII. Children of the Marriage

While Zack and Skye were both raised as Roman Catholics, neither Zack nor Skye practices Roman Catholicism nor subscribes to the principles of the Roman Catholic faith. Accordingly, Zack and Skye agree and acknowledge that it would *not* be in the best interests of any children they may have or adopt together to be raised according to the principles of the Roman Catholic faith. Zack and Skye further agree to raise any children they may have or adopt together with a healthy respect for all religions, but without any formal training in any particular religion.

Other than the foregoing provision, the parties do not wish to make any other provisions relating to any children born to them or adopted by them (including custody, visitation, and support). Nothing in this Agreement shall relieve a party of the obligation to pay the other support for any children born to or adopted by them.

XIX. Further Documents

The parties agree that, upon the request of the other or his/her legal representatives, they will each execute, acknowledge and deliver to the other or his/her legal representatives, as the case may be, any and all instruments appropriate or necessary to carry into effect the provisions of this Agreement.

This section addresses Skye's desire that their children not be raised as Roman Catholics.

Because parents cannot waive their children's right to support, this section confirms that the Agreement does not affect the issue of child support in any way.

Often, additional documents must be executed to effectuate the purposes of a prenuptial agreement. This section provides that Zack and Skye will sign whatever additional documents are necessary to put the provisions of the Agreement into effect.

XX. General Provisions

Both Zack and Skye acknowledge that this Agreement contains the entire understanding between them with respect to the terms of their divorce and that there are no agreements or understandings between them that are not specifically mentioned in the Agreement. Both Zack and Skye further agree that this Agreement supersedes any prior agreements, whether oral or in writing.

This Agreement may be modified only in writing, signed and acknowledged by both Zack and Skye. No oral modifications of the Agreement may be made.

If either Zack or Skye fails to insist upon strict performance of any right or obligation under the Agreement, such failure shall not be construed as a waiver of his or her right to insist upon strict performance in the future and to seek remedies for any prior breach.

Each right and obligation under the Agreement is independent of any other paragraph or provision of the Agreement. If any paragraph or provision of this Agreement is deemed invalid for any reason, that shall not invalidate or in any way affect the remaining paragraphs and provisions of the Agreement.

This Agreement shall inure to the benefit of, and shall be binding upon, the parties hereto and their respective heirs, executors, administrators, and assigns.

This clause provides that there are no unwritten understandings between Zack and Skye on any issue relating to the prenuptial agreement.

This very important provision establishes that the terms of their prenuptial agreement may only be changed in writing. If Skye said to Zack that he could have half of her condominium, for example, Skye's statement would have no legal effect unless the two modified their prenuptial agreement in writing to reflect Skye's generosity.

Sometimes courts will strike down one or more provisions of a contract. In the rare event that any one provision of Zack and Skye's prenuptial agreement is nullified by a court, this clause ensures that the rest of their agreement will still stand.

To reduce incentives to challenge the prenuptial agreement down the line, this clause provides that the spouse who challenges the prenuptial agreement or refuses to comply with its terms must pay the other spouse's attorney's fees.

Any party who fails to comply with any provision or obligation contained in this Agreement shall pay the other party's attorney's fees, costs, and other expenses reasonably incurred in enforcing this Agreement and resulting from the noncompliance.

Any notices under this Agreement shall be sent by certified mail, return receipt requested and regular mail to the parties at the following addresses: to Zachary Michael Mitchell at 4 Willoughby Street, Apt. 2E, New York, New York 10023 and to Skye Ann Johnson residing at 25 Riverside Avenue, Apt. 4F, New York, New York 10021. Copies of such notices shall be sent by hand or by telecopier and regular mail to Zack's attorney, Anna Kraus, Esq., at Thacher & Wardwell, 425 Madison Avenue, New York, New York 10017 and to Skye's attorney, Nina Cohen, Esq., at Shearman & Skadden, 803 Third Avenue, New York, New York 10012.

Prenuptial agreements must be signed by both parties and usually must be notarized as well.

IN WITNESS WHEREOF, Zack and Skye have set their hands and seals to six counterparts of this Agreement, each of which shall constitute an original, this 19th day of November, 2004, in the city of New York, State of New York.

Zachary M. Mitchell
ZACHARY MICHAEL MITCHELL

Bob A. Smith
BOB A. SMITH

Skye Ann Johnson
SKYE ANN JOHNSON

Mary S. Smith
MARY S. SMITH

Acknowledgement
STATE OF NEW YORK)

                      ss:

COUNTY OF NEW YORK)

On this 19th day of November 2004, before me personally appeared ZACHARY MICHAEL MITCHELL, to me known and known to me to be the individual described in and who executed the within instrument, and he acknowledged to me that he executed the same.

John D. Public
NOTARY PUBLIC

Acknowledgement
STATE OF NEW YORK)

                      ss:

COUNTY OF NEW YORK)

On this 19th day of November 2004, before me personally appeared SKYE ANN JOHNSON, to me known and known to me to be the individual described in and who executed the within instrument, and she acknowledged to me that she executed the same.

John D. Public
NOTARY PUBLIC

8

After the Honeymoon: A Postscript about Postnups

So what happens if you have already gone ahead and tied the knot with your loved one? Believe it or not, you can *still* enter into an agreement with your spouse regarding your financial rights and responsibilities. Instead of a prenuptial agreement, however, you and your spouse will enter into a *postnuptial agreement*. Postnuptial agreements are very similar to prenuptial agreements. Just like a prenup, a postnup can establish each spouse's property rights in the event of debt, divorce, and death. A postnup can also address how money will be managed during your marriage. As is the case with prenups, postnups must be put down in writing and signed by both spouses. You and your spouse must provide one another with complete financial disclosure prior to entering into a postnup and neither of you can force the other to sign a postnup against his or her will. Just as you would each hire separate lawyers for the purposes of a prenup, you and your spouse should retain independent counsel to advise you on your rights with respect to your postnup.

An extremely important requirement for postnups—perhaps more so than for prenups—is that the agreement be fundamentally fair to both of you. Why? Because after the marriage has already taken place, the financially dependent spouse has far less leverage to negotiate for favorable terms.

EXAMPLE

Sebastian and his wife, Gwen, had been married for fifteen years when one of Sebastian's novels hit the bestseller list. All of a sudden, Sebastian was on *Oprah* and *Good Morning America*, and his murder mystery was flying off the bookstore shelves. Before his writing career met with this stroke of good fortune, Sebastian had been a struggling writer, someone who rejoiced every time he made a few hundred dollars for publishing a short story here and there. Sebastian and Gwen's marriage had been struggling along as well. He and Gwen did not get along nearly as well as they once had and they were in marriage counseling.

Once the royalty checks started to roll in, Sebastian decided to ask Gwen for a postnuptial agreement providing that his book proceeds would be considered his separate property in the event of a divorce. Gwen thought this was an incredibly unfair proposal. She had worked long hours as an emergency room nurse throughout their marriage and her comfortable salary had enabled Sebastian to spend his days holed up in his office with his notepads and coffee cups. Sebastian had hardly contributed anything at all financially for nearly fifteen years. Now, just when he was actually making a decent living, he wanted to cut her out of everything in the event of a divorce.

Gwen grappled with the decision for days, but ultimately agreed to sign the postnup Sebastian proposed after he threatened to divorce her. While Gwen knew that their marriage was a troubled one, she could not bear the thought of divorce. No one in her family had ever been divorced and starting life all over again at age 48 was not a real option for her. So Gwen gritted her teeth and signed the agreement, promising herself that she would spend everything she had to challenge the postnup if Sebastian ever filed for divorce and tried to enforce it.

Two years and three bestsellers later, Sebastian left Gwen for his literary agent. Predictably, Sebastian claimed that he owed Gwen nothing since the terms of their postnup provided that his enormous book royalties were off-limits. Gwen was steaming. She took out a huge loan against her 401(k) and used it to pay the retainer fee for the city's best divorce lawyer. Gwen's lawyer challenged the postnup on the grounds that Sebastian had forced Gwen to sign the agreement against her will by threatening to divorce her. Gwen won and Sebastian had to fork over nearly half of his hefty royalty checks. What's more, the court concluded that the novels themselves were marital property (since they were written during the marriage). So Sebastian had to share all of his *future* royalty checks with Gwen as well!

The moral of this story is that you should be *extremely* careful to make sure that your spouse signs your postnup of his or her own free will and that the terms of your postnup are fundamentally fair.

When to Consider a Postnup

A postnup can be a useful financial tool for almost any couple. However, you and your spouse should give serious thought to the idea of a postnuptial agreement if any of the following applies to your situation.

- ◆ *You and your spouse have recently contemplated divorce.* Having a postnup in place can allow you and your spouse to focus on the business of getting your marriage back on track without any lingering concerns about property division and spousal support in the event of a divorce.

◆ *You or your spouse has recently received a sizeable inheritance or gift from a relative or friend.* A postnuptial agreement can ensure that the inheritance or gift will remain *off limits* in the event of a divorce.

◆ *Your financial or professional circumstances have changed a great deal since you first got married.* If one of you has made significant career sacrifices for the other, or if one of you has become much more (or less) wealthy than you ever thought you would be, a postnuptial agreement can help guarantee that you and your spouse will each be treated fairly in the event of death or divorce.

◆ *You or your spouse took out a sizeable amount of debt or entered a high-liability profession during your marriage.* A postnuptial agreement can provide that each spouse is responsible for his or her own debt and can help to keep one spouse's assets safe from the other spouse's creditors.

Even if you and your spouse decide that a postnuptial agreement is not for you, the process of discussing your financial rights in the event of debt, divorce, and death is an extremely useful exercise in and of itself. Chances are, you and your spouse will walk away from the discussion with a better understanding of the other's views on important money matters—and as a result, you may even end up arguing less over money in the future.

Glossary

A

abandonment. When one spouse intentionally separates from the other spouse for a year or more, that spouse may be "guilty" of *abandonment*. (*Abandonment* is grounds for divorce in most states.)

abuse. See *spousal abuse*.

adultery. When one spouse engages in sexual relations with someone else, that spouse is "guilty" of *adultery*. (*Adultery* is grounds for divorce in most states.)

alimony. See *spousal support*.

appreciation. An increase in value. For example, if your company's stock grows from $10 per share to $20 per share, there has been a $10 per share *appreciation*.

B

bankruptcy. When your liabilities exceed your assets by a great deal, you may be able to file a petition for *bankruptcy* to have a court discharge some or all of your debts.

beneficiary. The person or entity you designate to receive assets or profits. For example, if you name your daughter as the *beneficiary* of your life insurance policy, she will receive the proceeds of the policy when you die.

beneficiary deed. Allows you to have your property pass directly to someone else in the event of your death, outside of the probate process.

bequest. A gift of personal property made in a will.

binding. A legally enforceable agreement. (An oral prenuptial agreement, for example, is not *binding.*)

Black-Scholes formula. A formula used to value stock options.

buy out. As the name suggests, the *buy out* method allows one person to *buy out* another person's share of marital property in a divorce.

buy-sell agreements. These agreements are designed to govern how much a business partner will receive as his or her share of a business or professional practice in the event that partner leaves the practice or business for any reason. They often place a dollar value on shares and/or business goodwill.

C

capitalization of earnings. A formula used to determine the value of a business by multiplying the annual earnings of the business by an appropriate capitalization factor.

capitalization of excess earnings. A formula used to place a dollar value on professional goodwill, by multiplying the amount the professional earns in excess of a similarly situated professional by an appropriate capitalization factor.

child support. When parents decide to separate or divorce, the noncustodial parent must provide the custodial parent with regular financial assistance—or *child support*—to help cover the expenses of raising the child. Each state has financial guidelines for determining the amount of child support.

closely held corporations. Corporations in which the shares are held by a small number of people. Because there is no public market for the shares, it can be difficult to value the shares of a closely-held corporation.

collection agency. An agency charged with the task of collecting unpaid debts.

commingle. The mixing of marital property with separate property. (*Commingling* can cause separate property to be treated as marital property in the event of a divorce.)

community property. The term refers to all property earned or acquired by either spouse during the marriage. (In states that follow the *community property* system, each spouse has a one-half interest in all *community property* from the moment the property is earned or acquired.)

conditional gift. One that comes with strings attached, so to speak. The perfect example is an engagement ring, which is conditional on marriage.

consolidate. If you have several debts of the same type (for example, credit card liabilities), you may be able to *consolidate* the debts into one debt to enjoy a lower interest rate or administrative convenience.

constructive abandonment. When one spouse refuses to have sexual relations with the other spouse for a period of one year or more, that spouse may be guilty of *constructive abandonment*. (*Constructive abandonment* is grounds for divorce in many states.)

contract. A legally binding agreement between two or more parties.

creditor. A person or entity to whom you owe money.

cruel and inhuman treatment. Severe emotional, physical, or sexual abuse. (*Cruel and inhuman treatment* is grounds for divorce in most states.)

custody. There are two types of *custody*. The parent with *primary physical custody* lives with the child on a day-to-day basis. The parent with *legal custody* has the right to make major medical, educational, and other decisions affecting the child.

D

deed. A title document specifying ownership of real estate.

devise. A gift of real estate made pursuant to a will.

disability insurance. A policy that pays benefits in the event that you cannot perform your job because of a health-related condition.

discharge. When you file a petition for bankruptcy, a bankruptcy court has the authority to free you from your debts by *discharging* them.

E

electing against the will. If you leave your spouse less than the amount of the elective share, your spouse may *elect against your will* to claim his or her full elective share of your estate.

elective share. The amount of your estate that your spouse is automatically entitled to receive, regardless of the provisions of your will.

enhanced earning capacity. One spouse's ability to earn money increases during the marriage (for example, if one spouse earns a professional degree).

equitable distribution. Most states divide marital property according to what is fair under the circumstances of the case, a system known as *equitable distribution.*

estate. The property you own when you die.

F

fault. See *marital fault.*

filing jointly. Married individuals have their choice of filing their tax returns jointly with their spouses or filing their taxes as *married filing separately.*

financial misconduct. In the context of divorce, refers to the wasting of marital property. For example, a husband who takes out a second mortgage on the marital home to purchase a diamond necklace for his lover would be guilty of *financial misconduct*.

foreclosure. The mortgage lender has the right to repossess your home in a *foreclosure* proceeding if your mortgage loan goes unpaid.

G

garnish. Lenders may collect unpaid debts by taking a portion of your income.

gift. A transfer of property to someone else. The word generally refers to transfers made while you are still alive.

goodwill. The reputation value of a business or professional practice.

grounds. The legal basis for a divorce.

H

high liability profession. Someone in a *high liability profession* is at greater risk of being sued for his or her professional conduct than other professionals. (For example, surgeons are in a *higher liability profession* than dentists.)

I

inheritance. Property received after someone's death.

intellectual property. Refers, generally, to inventions, written works, musical works, and artistic works.

intestate. If you die without a will, you will have died *intestate*.

intestate succession. When you do not leave instructions for how you would like the property in your estate to be distributed in the event of your death, the laws of *intestate succession* will govern the distribution of your estate.

irreconcilable differences. A no-fault ground for divorce in many states. (To obtain a divorce on grounds of *irreconcilable differences*, one spouse must simply claim that the marriage has broken down to the point that reconciliation is no longer possible.)

J
joint tenancy with rights of survivorship. Property automatically passes to the other joint tenant in the event of one tenant's death.

K
kitchen sink states. Some states consider all property owned by either spouse at the end of a marriage to constitute marital property, regardless of the source of the property.

L
legal separation. Allows a couple to live separate and apart from one another, and to apply to the court for relief such as property division and child support, without obtaining a formal decree of divorce.

liability. The legal responsibility for the consequences of your actions. (If you rear-end your neighbor's new Porsche, for example, you would be *liable* to your neighbor for the damages. The term *liability* is also used to describe debts. For example, if you take out a $200,000 mortgage, then you would have $200,000 in mortgage *liability*.)

life insurance. A contract whereby an insurance company will pay benefits to a designated beneficiary in the event of your death.

lifestyle provisions. Clauses in a prenuptial or postnuptial agreement that are unrelated to financial issues. (*Lifestyle provisions* are generally not enforced by courts.)

long-term care insurance. A contract whereby an insurance company will cover the costs of nursing home care or other extended care necessitated by old age or poor health.

M

maintenance. See *spousal support.*

margin loan. Allows someone to borrow against the value of his or her securities to purchase additional securities.

marital debt. The term refers to debt that is accrued during the marriage for marital purposes. (In a divorce, a court may allocate responsibility for *marital debt* between the spouses.)

marital estate. The term is often used to refer to all *marital property* owned by a couple. (For example, if a couple acquired a house, a car, and two retirement accounts during their marriage, then that property may collectively be referred to as the *marital estate.*)

marital fault. When one spouse cheats, abandons, or abuses the other, that spouse is guilty of *marital fault.* (Some state courts still take *marital fault* into account when making decisions about property division and spousal support.)

marital property. The term refers to the property that is divided between the spouses at the end of a marriage. (Subject to certain exceptions, all property earned or acquired during the marriage is generally considered *marital property.*)

marriage penalty. You and your spouse may end up owing a larger amount in taxes if you file jointly than you would have owed had you been single.

N

no-fault. This means that one spouse can successfully petition for a divorce even if the other spouse has been a model life partner.

P

pay on death (POD). See *transfer on death*.

pension. A sum of money paid on a regular basis to an employee when he or she reaches retirement age. (Instead of *pension* plans, many companies now offer 401(k) plans instead.)

permanent life insurance. *Permanent life insurance* provides life insurance coverage for the entire duration of your life, not just for a set period of time. The beneficiary of your *permanent life insurance* policy will be paid the benefits of the policy even if you die when you are one hundred years old.

personal guarantee. You are personally responsible for repaying a business-related loan—even if the business becomes insolvent.

personal injury. See *compensation for a personal injury*.

postnuptial agreement. An agreement entered into between spouses, after the marriage has already taken place.

premarital. The time before the marriage.

premarital agreement. See *prenuptial agreement*.

prenuptial. See *premarital*.

prenuptial agreement. A contract between prospective spouses (also known as a premarital agreement). Usually, a *prenuptial agreement* will specify each spouse's rights and obligations when it comes to death, divorce, and debts.

probate. The process whereby your debts are paid and your assets are distributed in accordance with the terms of your will.

probate estate. A *probate estate* consists of all property that passes through a will. (Property that passes outside of the probate process (such as life insurance) is not part of the *probate estate*.)

property division. The process by which marital property or community property is divided between spouses in a divorce.

Q
QDRO (Qualified Domestic Relations Order). Provides for the division of pension and other retirement benefits as and when they are actually paid.

QTIP trust (Qualified Terminable Interest Property trust). Allows one to leave property to someone (usually a spouse) while still retaining control over what happens to the property during that person's lifetime and after his or her death.

R
reimbursement alimony. When one spouse has made sacrifices to advance the other spouse's career, that spouse may be awarded *reimbursement alimony* as compensation.

S

separate property. Property is generally not divided between spouses in a divorce.

spousal abuse. When one spouse emotionally, physically, or sexually mistreats the other spouse. (*Spousal abuse* is grounds for divorce in most states.)

spousal support. When one spouse cannot provide for his or her own reasonable needs, a divorce court may order the other spouse to pay *spousal support* for a set period of time. (*Spousal support* may also be referred to as *alimony* or *maintenance*.)

stock option. The right to purchase or sell stock for a fixed price, which is usually very favorable compared to the stock's trading price.

strike price. The price at which a stock can be bought or sold pursuant to a stock option.

student loan. A loan to assist with tuition and other education-related expenses.

T

taking against the will. See *electing against the will*.

tax fraud. While everyone tries hard to minimize taxes, cutting down your tax bill illegally—for example, by underreporting your income—is considered *tax fraud*.

tax under-reporting. If you earn $100,000 but you only report $50,000 on your income tax return, then you are engaging in a form of tax fraud known as *tax underreporting*.

term life insurance. Insurance that provides life insurance coverage for only a set number of years. (For example, you might choose to purchase term life insurance that insures you until you are sixty-five, so that your kids will be protected if you die while you are still providing for them.)

testate. A person who dies with a will in place.

title. *Title* refers to the legal ownership of property. (For example, if you own a house in your name only, then you have *title* to the house.)

transfer on death (TOD). Permits property to be directly transferred to somebody else in the event of your death. (A key advantage of using such designations is that the property will not have to go through the probate process.)

trust. A legal device for transferring property. (Trusts are often used to provide limits on how and when the beneficiary may use the money in the trust.)

U

unvested. Often, employee benefits such as pension plans come with certain requirements (for example, many companies require that the employee remain with the company for a certain number of years to qualify for the benefit). When these conditions have not been met, the benefit is considered *unvested*. This means that the employee could lose the benefit if he or she leaves the company too soon or fails to meet some other requirement.

V

vested. When all of the necessary conditions to an employee benefit (such as stock options or a pension) have been met, the benefit is considered *vested*. This generally means that the employee can no longer lose the benefit.

visitation. When one parent is awarded custody, the other parent is generally entitled to see the child on a regular basis.

W

will. A legal document that specifies how your assets should be distributed in the event of your death.

State-by-State Summary of Probate Laws

The following is a very simplified summary of the probate laws of each state. Please bear in mind that what counts as the deceased spouse's estate for intestate and elective share purposes varies from state to state. Also note that some states grant spouses other estate rights, such as housing allowances, that are not listed on the chart. To understand exactly how the probate laws of your state work, you should consult with a trusts and estates attorney.

Alabama

Intestate Share   At least one-half of the deceased spouse's estate.

Elective Share   The lesser of one-third of the deceased spouse's estate or the deceased spouse's entire estate less the surviving spouse's separate estate.

Alaska

Intestate Share   At least the first $100,000 plus half of the remainder of the deceased spouse's estate.

Elective Share   One-third of the deceased spouse's estate.

Arizona

Intestate Share   At least one-half of the deceased spouse's estate.

Elective Share   One-half of the community property.

Arkansas

Intestate Share   At least one-third of the deceased spouse's estate.

Elective Share   At least one-third of the deceased spouse's estate.

California

Intestate Share   One-half of all community property and quasi-community property, plus at least one-third of the deceased spouse's separate property.

Elective Share   One-half of all community property and quasi-community property.

Colorado

Intestate Share   At least one-half of the deceased spouse's estate.

Elective Share   A sliding scale, depending on the length of the marriage.

Connecticut

Intestate Share   At least one-half of the deceased spouse's estate.

Elective Share   A life estate in one-third of the deceased spouse's property.

Delaware

Intestate Share   At least one-half of the deceased spouse's personal property and a life estate in the deceased spouse's real property.

Elective Share   One-third of the deceased spouse's estate.

District
of Columbia

Intestate Share   At least one-half of the deceased spouse's estate.

Elective Share   One-half of the deceased spouse's estate.

Florida

Intestate Share   At least one-half of the deceased spouse's estate.

Elective Share   30% of the deceased spouse's estate.

Georgia

Intestate Share   At least one-third of the deceased spouse's estate.

Elective Share   One year's support.

Hawaii

Intestate Share   At least the first $100,000 plus one-half of the remainder of the deceased spouse's estate.

Elective Share   3% (for one year of marriage) to 50% of the deceased spouse's estate, depending on the length of the marriage.

Idaho

Intestate Share   One-half of the community property plus at least one-half of the deceased spouse's separate property.

Elective Share   One-half of the community property.

Illinois

Intestate Share   At least one-half of the deceased spouse's estate.

Elective Share   At least one-third of the deceased spouse's estate.

Indiana

Intestate Share   At least one-half of the deceased spouse's estate.

Elective Share   At least one-third of the deceased spouse's personal estate, plus one-quarter of the deceased spouse's real estate.

Iowa

Intestate Share   At least the greater of $50,000 or one-half of the deceased spouse's personal property, plus all of the deceased spouse's personal property that is exempt from creditors' claims.

Elective Share   One-third of the deceased spouse's real property plus a portion of the deceased spouse's personal property.

Kansas

Intestate Share   At least one-half of the deceased spouse's estate.

Elective Share   3% (for one year of marriage) to 50% of the deceased spouse's estate, depending on the length of the marriage.

Kentucky

Intestate Share $15,000.

Elective Share   A life estate in one-third of the deceased spouse's estate plus one-half of the deceased spouse's personal property.

Louisiana

Intestate Share   Use of the deceased spouse's separate property.

Elective Share   One-half of all community property.

Maine

Intestate Share   At least one-half of the deceased spouse's estate.

Elective Share   One-third of the deceased spouse's estate.

Maryland

Intestate Share   At least one-half of the deceased spouse's estate.

Elective Share   At least one-third of the deceased spouse's estate.

Massachusetts

Intestate Share   At least one-half of the deceased spouse's estate.

Elective Share   At least one-third of the deceased spouse's estate.

Michigan

Intestate Share   At least one-half of the deceased spouse's estate.

Elective Share   One-half of the deceased spouse's estate.

Minnesota

Intestate Share   At least one-half of the deceased spouse's estate.

Elective Share   One-third of the deceased spouse's estate.

Mississippi

Intestate Share   The deceased spouse's estate is divided equally among the deceased spouse's children and the surviving spouse.

Elective Share   At least one-half of the deceased spouse's estate.

Missouri

Intestate Share   At least half of the deceased spouse's estate.

Elective Share   At least one-third of the deceased spouse's estate.

Montana

Intestate Share At least the first $100,000, plus one-half of the deceased spouse's estate.

Elective Share 3% (for one year of marriage) to 50% of the deceased spouse's estate, depending on the length of the marriage.

Nebraska

Intestate Share At least one-half of the deceased spouse's estate.

Elective Share One-half of the deceased spouse's estate.

Nevada

Intestate Share At least one-third of the deceased spouse's estate.

Elective Share A homestead allowance plus *reasonable* support.

New Hampshire

Intestate Share At least one-half of the deceased spouse's estate.

Elective Share At least one-third of the deceased spouse's estate.

New Jersey

Intestate Share At least one-half of the deceased spouse's estate.

Elective Share One-third of the deceased spouse's estate.

New Mexico

Intestate Share At least one-quarter of the deceased spouse's estate.

Elective Share One-half of the community property.

New York

Intestate Share $50,000 plus half of the remainder of the deceased spouse's estate.

Elective Share   At least one-third of the deceased spouse's estate.

North Carolina

Intestate Share   At least one-third of the deceased spouse's estate.

Elective Share   At least one-third of the deceased spouse's estate.

North Dakota

Intestate Share   At least the first $100,000 plus one-half of the remainder of the deceased spouse's estate.

Elective Share   One-half of the deceased spouse's estate.

Ohio

Intestate Share $20,000 plus at least one-third of the remainder of the deceased spouse's estate.

Elective Share   At least one-third of the deceased spouse's estate.

Oklahoma

Intestate Share   At least one-third of the deceased spouse's estate.

Elective Share   One-half of the deceased spouse's estate.

Oregon

Intestate Share   At least one-half of the deceased spouse's estate.

Elective Share   One-half of the deceased spouse's estate.

Pennsylvania

Intestate Share   At least one-half of the deceased spouse's estate.

Elective Share   One-third of the deceased spouse's estate.

Rhode Island

Intestate Share   A minimum of a life estate in the deceased spouse's real estate.

Elective Share   A minimum of a life estate in the deceased spouse's real estate.

South Carolina

Intestate Share   At least one-half of the deceased spouse's estate.

Elective Share   One-third of the deceased spouse's estate.

South Dakota

Intestate Share   At least the first $100,000 plus one-half of the remainder of the deceased spouse's estate.

Elective Share   3% (for one year of marriage) to 50% of the deceased spouse's estate, depending on the length of the marriage.

Tennessee

Intestate Share   At least one-third of the deceased spouse's estate.

Elective Share   A sliding scale, depending on the length of the marriage.

Texas

Intestate Share   At least one-third of the deceased spouse's personal property, plus a life estate in one-third of the deceased spouse's real property.

Elective Share   One-half of the community property.

Utah

Intestate Share   At least the first $100,000, plus one-half of the remainder of the deceased spouse's estate.

Elective Share   One-third of the deceased spouse's estate.

Vermont

Intestate Share   At least one-third of the deceased spouse's estate.

Elective Share   At least one-third of the deceased spouse's estate.

Virginia

Intestate Share   At least one-third of the deceased spouse's estate.

Elective Share   At least one-third of the deceased spouse's estate.

Washington

Intestate Share   All of the community property, plus at least one-half of the deceased spouse's separate property.

Elective Share   One-half of the community property.

West Virginia

Intestate Share   At least one-half of the deceased spouse's estate.

Elective Share   3% to 50% of the deceased spouse's estate, depending on the length of the marriage.

Wisconsin

Intestate Share   At least one-half of the deceased spouse's estate.

Elective Share   One-half of the marital property.

Wyoming

Intestate Share   At least one-half of the deceased spouse's estate.

Elective Share   At least one-quarter of the deceased spouse's estate.

State-by-State Summary of Divorce Laws

Because the divorce laws are rather complicated, this table simply identifies the general structure of each state's marital property classification and division systems. A state that adheres to a *dual property system* for the classification of marital property strictly distinguishes between marital property (such as income earned during the marriage) and separate property (such as inheritance funds). A state that follows the *hybrid system* for the classification of marital property will only divide marital property in the event of a divorce, unless it would be unjust not to divide the separate property as well, given the facts of the case.

Finally, a state that follows the *kitchen sink system* of marital property classification considers all property that a couple owns to constitute marital property, regardless of the origin of that property. You will see from the chart that divorce courts in a number of states are still technically permitted to take marital fault into account when making property division and spousal support decisions. As a practical matter, however, courts in most (but not all) states place very little weight on marital fault when making financial awards. To understand exactly how the divorce laws of your state work, consult with a matrimonial attorney.

Alabama

Marital Property Classification Dual property system.

Marital Property Division Equitable distribution.

Spousal Support The court may take marital fault into account.

Alaska

Marital Property Classification Hybrid system.

Marital Property Division Equitable distribution, with a presumption of equal division.

Spousal Support Marital fault is not a factor for consideration.

Arizona

Marital Property Classification Dual property system.

Marital Property Division Equitable distribution.

Spousal Support Marital fault is not a factor for consideration.

Arkansas

Marital Property Classification	Hybrid system.
Marital Property Division	Equal division, unless an equal division would be inequitable given the circumstances of the case.
Spousal Support	Marital fault is not a factor for consideration.

California

Marital Property Classification	Dual property system.
Marital Property Division	Equal division.
Spousal Support	Marital fault is not a factor for consideration.

Colorado

Marital Property Classification	Dual property system.
Marital Property Division	Equitable distribution.
Spousal Support	Marital fault is not a factor for consideration.

Connecticut

Marital Property Classification   Kitchen sink system.

Marital Property Division   Equitable distribution. The court may take marital fault into account.

Spousal Support   The court may take marital fault into account.

Delaware

Marital Property Classification   Dual property system.

Marital Property Division   Equitable distribution.

Spousal Support   Marital fault is not a factor for consideration.

District of Columbia

Marital Property Classification   Dual property system.

Marital Property Division   Equitable distribution. The court may take marital fault into account.

Spousal Support   The court may take marital fault into account.

Florida

Marital Property Classification   Dual property system.

Marital Property Division   Equal division, unless an equal division would be inequitable given the circumstances of the case.

Spousal Support   The court may take marital fault into account.

Georgia

Marital Property Classification   Dual property system.

Marital Property Division   Equitable distribution.

Spousal Support   The court may take marital fault into account.

Hawaii

Marital Property Classification   Kitchen sink system.

Marital Property Division   Equitable distribution. The court may take marital fault into account.

Spousal Support   The court may take marital fault into account.

Idaho

Marital Property Classification

Dual property system.

Marital Property Division

Equal division, unless an equal division would be inequitable given the circumstances of the case.

Spousal Support

The court may take marital fault into account.

Illinois

Marital Property Classification

Dual property system.

Marital Property Division

Equitable distribution.

Spousal Support

Marital fault is not a factor for consideration.

Indiana

Marital Property Classification

Kitchen sink system.

Marital Property Division

Equal division, unless an equal division would be inequitable given the circumstances of the case.

Spousal Support

Marital fault is not a factor for consideration.

Iowa

Marital Property Classification	Hybrid system.
Marital Property Division	Equitable distribution.
Spousal Support	Marital fault is not a factor for consideration.

Kansas

Marital Property Classification	Kitchen sink system.
Marital Property Division	Equitable distribution.
Spousal Support	Marital fault is not a factor for consideration.

Kentucky

Marital Property Classification	Dual property system.
Marital Property Division	Equitable distribution.
Spousal Support	Marital fault is not a factor for consideration.

Louisiana

Marital Property Classification	Dual property system.
Marital Property Division	Equal division.
Spousal Support	The court may take marital fault into account.

Maine

Marital Property Classification

Dual property system.

Marital Property Division

Equitable distribution.

Spousal Support

Marital fault is not a factor for consideration.

Maryland

Marital Property Classification

Dual property system.

Marital Property Division

Equitable distribution. The court may take marital fault into account.

Spousal Support

The court may take marital fault into account.

Massachusetts

Marital Property Classification

Kitchen sink system.

Marital Property Division

Equitable distribution.

Spousal Support

The court may take marital fault into account.

Michigan

Marital Property Classification

Dual property system.

Marital Property Division

Equitable distribution.

Spousal Support

The court may take marital fault into account.

Minnesota

Marital Property Classification

The court may take marital fault into account.

Marital Property Division

Equitable distribution.

Spousal Support

Marital fault is not a factor for consideration.

Mississippi

Marital Property Classification

Dual property system.

Marital Property Division

Equitable distribution. The court may take marital fault into account.

Spousal Support

The court may take marital fault into account.

Missouri

Marital Property Classification

Dual property system.

Marital Property Division

Equitable distribution. The court may take marital fault into account.

Spousal Support

The court may take marital fault into account.

Montana

Marital Property Classification

Kitchen sink system.

Marital Property Division

Equitable distribution.

Spousal Support

Marital fault is not a factor for consideration.

Nebraska

Marital Property Classification

Dual property system.

Marital Property Division

Equitable distribution.

Spousal Support

Marital fault is not a factor for consideration.

Nevada

Marital Property Classification

Dual property system.

Marital Property Division

Equal division, unless an equal division would be inequitable given the circumstances of the case.

Spousal Support

Marital fault is not a factor for consideration.

New Hampshire

Marital Property Classification	Kitchen sink system.
Marital Property Division	Equitable distribution, with a presumption of equal division.
Spousal Support	The court may take marital fault into account.

New Jersey

Marital Property Classification	Dual property system.
Marital Property Division	Equitable distribution.
Spousal Support	The court may take marital fault into account.

New Mexico

Marital Property Classification	Dual property system.
Marital Property Division	Equal division.
Spousal Support	Marital fault is not a factor for consideration.

New York

Marital Property Classification	Dual property system.
Marital Property Division	Equitable distribution.
Spousal Support	The court may take marital fault into account.

North Carolina

Marital Property Classification

Dual property system.

Marital Property Division

Equal division, unless an equal division would be inequitable given the circumstances of the case.

Spousal Support

The court may take marital fault into account.

North Dakota

Marital Property Classification

Kitchen sink system.

Marital Property Division

Equitable distribution.

Spousal Support

The court may take marital fault into account.

Ohio

Marital Property Classification

Dual property system.

Marital Property Division

Equal division, unless an equal division would be inequitable given the circumstances of the case.

Spousal Support

Marital fault is not a factor for consideration.

Oklahoma

Marital Property Classification	Dual property system.
Marital Property Division	Equitable distribution.
Spousal Support	Marital fault is not a factor for consideration.

Oregon

Marital Property Classification	Kitchen sink system.
Marital Property Division	Equitable distribution.
Spousal Support	Marital fault is not a factor for consideration.

Pennsylvania

Marital Property Classification	Dual property system.
Marital Property Division	Equitable distribution.
Spousal Support	The court may take marital fault into account.

Rhode Island

Marital Property Classification	Dual property system.
Marital Property Division	Equitable distribution. The court may take marital fault into account.
Spousal Support	The court may take marital fault into account.

South Carolina

Marital Property Classification	Dual property system.
Marital Property Division	Equitable distribution. The court may take marital fault into account.
Spousal Support	The court may take marital fault into account.

South Dakota

Marital Property Classification	Kitchen sink system.
Marital Property Division	Equitable distribution.
Spousal Support	The court may take marital fault into account.

Tennessee

Marital Property Classification	Dual property system.
Marital Property Division	Equitable distribution.
Spousal Support	The court may take marital fault into account.

Texas

Marital Property Classification	Dual property system.
Marital Property Division	Equitable distribution.
Spousal Support	The court may take marital fault into account.

Utah

Marital Property Classification	Dual property system.
Marital Property Division	Equal division, unless an equal division would be inequitable given the circumstances of the case.
Spousal Support	The court may take marital fault into account.

Vermont

Marital Property Classification	Kitchen sink system.
Marital Property Division	Equitable distribution. The court may take marital fault into account.
Spousal Support	Marital fault is not a factor for consideration.

Virginia

Marital Property Classification	Dual property system.
Marital Property Division	Equitable distribution. The court may take marital fault into account.
Spousal Support	The court may take marital fault into account.

Washington

Marital Property Classification   Dual property system.

Marital Property Division   Equitable distribution.

Spousal Support   Marital fault is not a factor for consideration.

West Virginia

Marital Property Classification   Dual property system.

Marital Property Division   Equal division, unless an equal division would be inequitable given the circumstances of the case.

Spousal Support   The court may take marital fault into account.

Wisconsin

Marital Property Classification   Hybrid system.

Marital Property Division   Equal division, unless an equal division would be inequitable given the circumstances of the case.

Spousal Support   Marital fault is not a factor for consideration.

Wyoming

Marital Property Classification	Dual property system.
Marital Property Division	Equitable distribution. The court may take marital fault into account.
Spousal Support	The court may take marital fault into account.

Index

About the Author

Nihara K. Choudhri, Esq. is a graduate of Columbia Law School. She is the author of *The Complete Guide to Divorce Law* (Kensington Books 2004), and the divorce law expert for ivillage.com.

When she's not busy writing and lawyering, Nihara spends her time chasing her toddler son, Aman, through Central Park. She and her husband, Trin, have been married for seven years—and they hope to be blessed with seventy more wonderful years together.

Nihara has a few simple words of wisdom for soon-to-be-newlyweds:

Plan for every possibility, but hope for the very best—
and may the joys of your married life exceed even your wildest expectations.